NO DIET
WEIGHT LOSS

PAT WALDER

D1341062

Wellhouse Publishing Ltd

First published in Great Britain in 2003 by
Wellhouse Publishing Ltd
31 Middle Bourne Lane
Lower Bourne
Farnham
Surrey GU10 3NH

Reprinted in 2004, 2007, 2009

DISCLAIMER

The aim of this book is to provide general information only and
should not be treated as a substitute for the medical advice of
your doctor or any other health care professional. The publisher
and author are not responsible or liable for any diagnosis made
by a reader based on the contents of this book. Always consult
your doctor if you are in any way concerned about your health.

A catalogue record for this book is available from the British Library

ISBN 978-1 903784-10-5

Printed and bound by Ashford Colour Press Ltd., Fareham Road,
Gosport, Hampshire PO13 0FW.

Contents

Foreword

This book is full of common sense and good advice on how to change one's life permanently to overcome all the habits that produce obesity. I will certainly recommend it to my patients. It gives people an excellent insight into themselves and how they have become overweight. It gives rational and sound advice on how to change their attitudes and lifestyle, not just so that they can be thinner, but happier with themselves, too. And it does this in a style that is easy to read, with humour and sympathy. An excellent book for everyone involved in obesity - and nowadays that means more than half of the adult population. I wish I had written it myself.

Dr Tom Smith

About the Author

Pat Walder moved to London from Newcastle at the age of four. Her education included time at Hurlingham Technical College and Hammersmith College of Art. After spending four years as a Dental Nurse she then trained as a Nurse doing maternity and geriatric nursing. Pat trained in Hypnotherapy & Psychotherapy at the National Council of Psychotherapists and continued her training at The International Association of Hypno-Analysts. Following her training Pat became a founder member of the Wiltshire Academy of Hypnotherapy and Psychotherapy, this is a degree training course.

Pat is now connected with a Salisbury (Wiltshire) Therapy Centre, gives lectures and day seminars to insurance companies, recruitment organisations and large businesses on goal setting, stress management, and increasing wealth. Pat's main speciality is now Weight Control, she gives talks to large and small groups on this subject.

Introduction:

No Diet Weight Loss

I used to be a nurse, and often wondered why some patients would have illness after illness, often different illnesses, and yet others would never visit a doctor or hospital from one year to the next. I also used to wonder why some people would put on weight while others seemed to be able to eat anything in sight and never gain an ounce.

I once asked a doctor why, as our bodies were made in the same way, one person would become fat and another would remain slim, even though they ate relatively the same amounts and types of food. He explained about metabolic rates, enzymes and other things. I questioned him further and asked, 'But why would the enzymes in one person function differently from those in another?' This is where the conversation came to a halt. It seemed there was no answer. I was told it was 'just one of those things', 'something one was born with'. I found this most unsatisfactory, as I still had no idea why one person should be born with a different metabolism from another.

I later found that this was not the case.

I came to the conclusion that it must be something in the mind rather than the body that caused certain people to gain weight or fall ill more easily than others. I subsequently discovered that, more than anything else, weight is controlled by the way people think: their belief systems, attitudes and character.

The mind is inextricably linked to the body. The two cannot be separated. Anything that affects the mind must have an impact on the body, although some doctors (fewer these days) still see us as a load of spare parts that need servicing, and seem to ignore the part played by the mind.

The side-effects of some of the drugs used were causing more problems in some cases than the illnesses they were supposed to treat.

My discoveries led me to a search for more effective remedies to combat illness, based on the link between the body and the mind.

In those days I specialized in cancer therapy. In my search for the psychological reasons behind why some people would manifest physical problems while others developed psychological symptoms (such as phobias, panic attacks, eating problems and so on), I discovered some amazing facts.

It became clear to me that obesity had little to do with bad eating habits. It had more to do with other factors in the subconscious part of the mind, which began in infancy. Babies cry for many reasons, but it is usual for food to be offered as a first resort. The subconscious part of the mind then links emotional stress - feeling ill, feeling lonely, or needing a cuddle - with consuming food. When the baby is being fed he experiences the human contact he needs - which results in his no longer feeling lonely, afraid or abandoned. This, then, is a demonstration of an early erroneous belief being programmed into the mind which then causes a problem of being overweight in later life.

I then trained as a psychotherapist and hypnoanalyst, as these skills focus on an understanding of how the mind works. I have been an analyst for the past 14 years. The majority of clients who come to me have a weight problem. They are disillusioned from trying diet after diet and getting nowhere. After therapy, many of them use terms such as 'revolutionary', 'miraculous' and 'mind-blowing' when they lose pound after pound easily and naturally, without dieting or spending hours jogging round the park in the early hours. They have asked me to put the help I give them into a book. So here it is. Enough about me! Now let's discuss *your* problem.

There are many reasons why one individual will pile the weight on just by looking at a chocolate bar and another can eat everything in sight and never gain an ounce. *You* will be one of the latter group. What you will read in this book could change your life. You won't go on that eternal yo-yo of gaining and losing weight, only to find that after yet another diet, you weigh even more than you did before you began. You won't feel the sense of failure when, after deciding you would 'really stick to it this time', you find it 'impossible'.

DIETS DO NOT WORK.

Let's go a stage further.

DIETS MAKE YOU FAT!

You start to diet with great determination, and you begin to lose weight. But your protective mechanism - or, called by another name, your subconscious mind (which is the part of your mind that works on auto-pilot) - gets anxious and protects you by going into starvation mode, storing up any excess fat it can find. Inevitably, the weight loss stops. The dreaded plateau has been reached and you get disheartened. You then abandon the diet, and the pounds pile back on.

Your subconscious, meanwhile, remains a little anxious, in case the same thing happens again. It fears there may be another famine. So it keeps watch on the proceedings and maintains a little of the starvation mode. You start the next diet, and your subconscious snaps into a more severe starvation pattern.

Each time you go on a diet, your protective mechanism goes a little deeper into the starvation mode. You lose some. You gain some. You lose some and you gain even more. Eventually you have more excess fat than you had before you ever embarked on any diets. Your self-esteem is at rock bottom because you have proved to yourself again what a failure you are.

Diets really don't work. If they did, there would be no overweight people. The moment you tell yourself that you shouldn't eat something, you increase your desire for that very thing. Human nature being what it is, you crave that which you think you can't have.

People continually seek pleasure and avoid pain. We are programmed to do this, as a survival instinct. If we associate more pain than pleasure with dieting, we will inevitably abandon any diet. The survival instinct dictates that we will never achieve the perfect body-weight/height : ratio if it is based on how much pain we experience by depriving ourselves of something we want and which we would normally associate with pleasure (*for example, chocolate*).

This is what I mean by a *belief system*. If we can turn this around, and find ways of associating pain with eating that chocolate and becoming fat, and pleasure in being the perfect body weight and full of energy and vitality, and having high self-esteem, then we are on the way to achieving our goal. You will be shown how to do this later in this book.

When you cut down the amount you eat, for a while (and because the pleasure of being the ideal body weight is high at this point) you lose weight. But then you reach that plateau when you seem to be eating no more than would keep a fly alive but still those pounds won't shift. You lose heart (in other words, associate more pain than

pleasure with depriving yourself) and away you go on a binge of cho-
colate or whatever your particular bag is. On go the pounds again.
Eventually you weigh more than before you started the damned diet.
That's the bad news. Now for the good news.

STOP DOING WHAT DOES NOT WORK!

If you have now accepted totally that dieting does not work, I can
show you something that works extremely well. The first thing you
must do is give up on all those diets - unless you have a medical problem and are on a particular regime under medical supervision.

Abandon the search for the perfect diet. It does not exist. Tell yourself that you can eat whatever you wish from now on. If you follow the
suggestions in this book - and it doesn't take one ounce of will-power
on your part - you will discover, to your delight, that you just do not
want to eat the amounts or the same things that you did before, and
your weight will slide off without effort. You will also find that you can
maintain your perfect weight - and it will be easier than you ever
thought possible.

You will be unlikely to find the information contained in this book
anywhere else, as so many organizations have a vested interest in
keeping you overweight.

DOES THIS SOUND TOO GOOD TO BE TRUE?
THEN READ ON!

Chapter One

Making a Change

There are three basic rules that you need to keep in mind for the No Diet Weight Loss plan to work for you:

1. Eat slowly.
2. Chew thoroughly.
3. Notice the taste of everything that goes into your mouth.

If you develop these three habits you will eventually be the perfect body weight for your height.

I will explain why these three things are vital, because when you understand them fully it is much easier to stick to them and develop them as the necessary habits of a lifetime.

Eat Slowly

You have a gland inside your head called the hypothalamus. This gland controls your appetite and will give the 'full-up' signal approximately 20 minutes after you begin to eat. It does not matter how much or how little you have eaten in that time. If you eat quickly, you will put more food into your system in this time. If you eat slowly, you will put less food into your system in the 20 minutes before the full-up signal clicks into gear. When you eat slowly, you will have eaten far less than usual within that 20-minute period, yet you will still feel satisfied.

To prove to yourself that this is true, I recommend that you go to any café or restaurant and just look around at the diners. You will find that in almost every case the overweight diners are eating far more quickly than the thinner ones, who are eating at a much more leisurely pace. Don't take my word for it. Check it out for yourself, because when you see it you will believe it.

Now, let's look at why you developed bad eating habits at your mother's knee. Yes! We are blaming the parents, as usual.

As a child, you assumed that adults were always right. You also automatically took notice of the full-up signal by ceasing to eat when you had consumed enough food for your body to use as fuel. Then mother would probably say, 'Be a good girl/boy and eat up all your dinner.' So, being 'good' - for the child you were - meant eating more than you needed. After a while you assumed adults must be right in what they said as they had been on this planet a lot longer than you; so they must know everything. Right?

WRONG!

You then began to ignore your natural signals and do what you were told, to please the adults around you. You formed the view that you were supposed to eat until you felt uncomfortably full. Don't forget that you were totally dependent on others at this stage, as there was not a lot you could do for yourself.

Your parents, meanwhile, may have had doubts about their parenting abilities and may have also been concerned that you were not eating enough. They may have been children themselves during or after the war years, when rationing was in force. At this time, no one was ever sure when there would be another meal, so it was a good idea to eat as much as possible while food was available. Habits then get passed on from parent to child - after all, if it was good enough for your parents it must be good enough for you. Right?

WRONG!

Many people eat whenever they are upset or feeling alone and unloved, whether they are genuinely hungry or not. Let's see where *this* habit came from. Again, it was possibly learned in infancy.

When a child cries, it can be for many reasons. She may need her nappy changing, feel lonely, be scared, be in pain or just need a cuddle. But what happens? Parents and carers assume she is hungry and offer a bottle or food. The subconscious takes this programming on board: whenever there is an uncomfortable feeling, food is the answer. In later life, when the adult feels alone and unloved, or stressed or scared, eating has become an automatic reaction.

Chew Thoroughly

Your autonomic nervous system produces acid to process any food introduced into the system to be used as fuel. If you consume more food than the acid can cope with, it will process what it can; the rest will be stored as fat to be used later as needed.

The subconscious part of your mind which controls appetite is there for your survival, and always prepares for famine. Fuel is stored for this reason, mainly in the stomach area, which is why tummy fat is the hardest to shift.

Incidentally, have you ever wondered why your stomach muscles seem to be the most difficult to keep firm? If you think about it, most of the other muscles in your body are used continually throughout the day. Your biceps (upper-arm muscles) when you comb your hair, put food into your mouth, etc. Your leg muscles for sitting, standing, walking. Your neck muscles for turning your head. But your stomach muscles are rarely used in normal day-to-day living.

Whenever you take a walk it is a good idea to get used to holding your tummy muscles tight. In this way you equate walking with tightening these muscles, and eventually it becomes a habit.

But back to chewing thoroughly. If you consume less food, the acid will process this food and any acid that is left will begin to work on the fat stores. You then get a feeling of being hungry. Once this is understood, that feeling becomes a *good* feeling ('I'm losing fat') rather than a *bad* feeling ('Gosh, I'm hungry').

It is not a good idea, however, to leave yourself with this feeling for a great length of time as, when the fat has been processed, the acid may start to work on the stomach wall and you could develop an ulcer. Another possibility is that, again, when the fat stores have gone, the acid could begin working on your muscles. Having said this, as you have an interest in this book, you probably have a fair way to go before all your stored fat will be used up.

By chewing thoroughly you are doing most of the processing at mouth level, so there is less work for the acid, which can then begin on the fat stores more rapidly.

Notice the Taste of Everything that Goes into Your Mouth

You would think that noticing the taste of foods and drinks would increase your desire for them. It may do this at first, but there is a far more beneficial aspect to noticing tastes.

Your subconscious mind has a memory - so, for example, when you find yourself fancying something, chocolate for example, your memory is of something smooth, sweet, creamy and chocolatey, you never fancy something you have never had. If you currently eat it while watching television or reading a book, you are failing to notice the taste and so you are not satisfying the subconscious memory. As a result, even when you have eaten a whole bar, you may fancy some more.

If instead you start to savour the taste when eating, you are likely to satisfy the taste memory by the time you have eaten just a small amount. As with the no-diet plan you will no longer be telling yourself you must not have chocolate, you will be perfectly happy to put the rest away for another time.

Try this exercise to prove to yourself how strong your subconscious memory really is. Stand with your weight on one hip. Let your shoulders hunch forward. Then let the muscles in your face droop downward, with the sides of your mouth and eyes also drooping. Now try to feel happy. Impossible, isn't it? Now do the opposite. Stand up straight, shoulders back, head high. Put a huge smile on your face and try to feel miserable.

Your subconscious remembers that, in the past, whenever you stood in these stances you felt either happy or sad. So now, whenever you stand in these ways, your feelings and emotions will mirror your body language.

Which came first, the chicken or the egg? Or put another way, does standing in a drooping posture bring on a feeling of misery, or does the feeling of misery make you stand in a droopy way?

The answer is **BOTH!**

Armed with this knowledge, whenever you feel miserable all you have to do is stand in a happy position. Within a few minutes your insides will match your outside and you will feel full of joy and happiness.

You will get much more out of this book than the ability to lose weight. There will be many snippets of information such as this scattered throughout the book and, if you put these gems into practice, not only will you be slim and sylph-like, but much more confident and happy too.

Chapter Two

Helping Yourself

The information in this chapter is of paramount importance to the success of your weight program and to your enjoyment and success in all areas of your life.

Your subconscious mind enjoys the good emotions, such as joy, happiness, pride, achievement, a feeling of importance and so on. Your subconscious will do all it can to encourage these emotions. It dislikes the negative emotions such as guilt, shame, anger, feelings of futility and failure etc., and will do all in its power to escape these emotions.

Every time you remember to keep to the three rules of:

1. eating slowly
2. chewing thoroughly
3. noticing the taste of everything

always give yourself a pat on the back. Tell yourself how well you are doing, and feel good about your achievements. Your subconscious likes these feelings and will be more likely to use its resources to get more of them. In so doing it will assist you in remembering the three rules until the process becomes a habit.

The other side of the coin is this. Your subconscious does not like the negative emotions. It will do all in its power to avoid the feelings of pain, failure, guilt, shame, etc. If, every time you forget to utilize the three rules, you reproach yourself and tell yourself you are useless and will never remember, your subconscious will help you to avoid these unpleasant, negative feelings by making sure you forget more and more until you abandon the project.

Everything you have ever been, done, thought, tasted, experienced or felt is stored in your subconscious mind, which uses a filter system to bring to the conscious mind that which is needed at the time.

If, for example, when taking an exam you have read the information you need, it is all stored in the subconscious - whether you consciously remember it all or not. If you then go into that examination room thinking to yourself, 'I am never going to pass this exam', your subconscious will not bother to filter the information you need to the forefront of the brain. If, on the other hand, you go in feeling 'I will pass this exam easily: it is going to be a doddle', you are more likely to pass, as your subconscious knows that you expect the information to arrive when you need it. You will read the questions and the answers will automatically be there. They will just pop into your mind - rather like your telephone number or any information you care to access.

Think of other areas in your life where you unconsciously sabotage your own success by negative thinking, first by telling yourself it's not worth carrying on the struggle to achieve whatever you were trying to achieve at the time (fear of failure), and then by abandoning the project, just as it was likely to come to fruition, in case you should fail or the results not live up to your expectations. It is quite normal to do this, unconsciously, to avoid the risk of failing, so you abandon the project to escape that feeling. You cannot feel a failure if you do not finish properly what you started out to achieve. You have simply not finished. You can then rest secure in the belief that, if you *had* carried on, you would have succeeded. So it wasn't really a failure.

Alternatively, you could, of course, blame all and sundry for being unable to complete a task. For example: 'I can't stick to this diet as my early conditioning was of mother insisting I eat all the food on my plate.' Are you still living with your mother? If not, why are you blaming her for what you are doing now? Early conditioning *can* be a reason for failure, but only for the time when the conditioning is contained at an unconscious level. Once you are consciously aware of it, you have choices. It can no longer be effective and is being used as an excuse. Merely making the statement to yourself or others that your mother is to blame for your weight because of things she did when you were a child shows that you are consciously aware of the conditioning, so it can no longer apply, except as an excuse.

Speeding Up the Process

If you have now begun the process of eating slowly, chewing thoroughly, and noticing the taste of all food and drink you consume, you should be on the way to a slimmer you. What follows gives ways to speed up the process. It is a good idea for you to decide that you need only instigate the following instructions for a maximum of three weeks. If you plan to do them for the rest of your life, you might well fall at the first hurdle. It is important that you can visualize an end-goal.

The 10 suggestions in the next chapter serve two important purposes:

a)They are mostly ways to fool your subconscious into thinking you have eaten more than you actually have (as the subconscious has no way of knowing when you have satisfied your system's requirements for fuel).

It takes approximately four hours for a solid to be fully absorbed into the system, and about 20 minutes for a liquid. You would need to eat for about four hours if the subconscious gave the 'full-up' signal only when your stomach was full.

b)The other reason why these suggestions work, if put into practice, is that they empower you to make choices. You need no longer tell yourself you cannot have chocolate, cream cakes, etc., and so you are not increasing your desire for these things. You can have whatever you like, provided you carry out the following suggestions.

- *Praise yourself when you remember*
- *Don't reproach yourself when you forget*
- *Remember that everything is stored in the subconscious*
- *Expect success - create success*
- *Visualize an end-goal*

Chapter Three

Ten Steps to Freedom

1. Chart your progress
2. Decide on a place to eat
3. Set out a plate, knife and fork
4. When eating, do only that
5. Chew each mouthful thoroughly
6. Dine, don't shovel
7. Feel pride, not guilt, when disposing of unwanted food
8. Don't shop for food when you are hungry
9. Find a picture of yourself as you wish to be
10. Visualize yourself as the right body weight now

1. Chart Your Progress

If I had my way, I would abolish the sale of all scales for dieters, as scales cannot tell you how much fat-to-muscle you are carrying, nor how much water is in your system.

Suppose you weighed yourself first thing on Monday morning and found you weighed 'X' pounds. Then you religiously stuck to the rules of this book for three days. You then weighed yourself on Thursday morning and found the scales showed you had gained two pounds. You would be disheartened. You would be likely to give up. But don't! Let's examine what could have caused this weight increase.

On Monday morning you woke up. You visited the lavatory and emptied your bowels and bladder. You had not had a morning cup of tea and it had been a warm night, so your nightwear was of a light material. You got on the scales and noted the weight.

On Thursday morning, you woke and had two cups of tea, your bladder and bowel were full. It was a little chilly so you were wearing warmer, thicker nightwear. Maybe you were even premenstrual and were suffering from water retention. Is it any wonder the scales showed the extra pounds? But the extra pounds are not fat.

You can prove this to yourself right now. Stand on a set of scales and note your weight. Now drink a pint of water and weigh yourself again. You will have gained over a pound in weight, *but it is only the weight of the water*, and this will be disposed of as either urine or perspiration over the course of the day.

If you really must weigh yourself, then I suggest you do this no more than once a week, on the same day, and strictly under the same conditions. It is a much better idea to judge how well you are doing by noticing how your clothes seem to be getting looser, or seeing your appearance change in the mirror.

The following chart will enable you to map your progress by measurement rather than by the numbers on the scales. Measure the relevant areas of your body and write the measurements in the appropriate place. Do this now. At the end of the three-week period, notice the difference.

	Week one	Week two	Week three
Upper arms			
Calves			
Thighs			
Under bust/chest			
Full bust/chest			
Waist			
Hips			
Ankles			

2. Decide on a Place to Eat

Pick a place to eat (dining-room table, kitchen, etc.) and eat *only in that place*. Make sure that the place where you decide to eat has no television or other distractions. It will be almost impossible to concentrate on eating slowly, chewing thoroughly and noticing the taste of whatever you are consuming if you are engrossed in your favourite 'soap' on television.

This does not mean that, if you fancy your favourite treat while out shopping, you cannot buy it. It simply means that you would need to take it to your chosen place to eat. In this way, you are not telling yourself that you cannot have that treat. You are simply making choices.

I, personally, never have chocolate, cakes or biscuits in the house. I can have them if I choose, but would have to go to the corner shop or supermarket to purchase them. As I am basically lazy, I would only bother to do this if I really needed to eat this type of food. And sometimes, at least, it will prove to be not worth the effort.

Imagine you are watching your favourite programme on television and you are offered a sweet or a biscuit and you know you will have to go to your 'place' to eat it. Are you going to miss some of your programme, or will you decide to wait until it has finished, by which time you may have forgotten about the food on offer? Again, you are not telling yourself you must not have whatever food you want. You are making choices.

You may need two places to eat if you are at work all day. In which case, you would probably have one place at home and another for your lunch at work. But don't allow yourself to have one place at home, another when the sandwich trolley comes round at break time, another in the staff canteen, and yet another at the cake shop on the way home. You will only be fooling yourself.

3. Set Out a Plate, Knife and Fork

Even if you are only eating some peanuts, or a biscuit, laying a place setting helps you, again, to make choices. Since you are not telling yourself you must not have the food, you eliminate the increase in desire for that food.

Imagine someone at work offers you a biscuit. To eat it you will need to set out a plate, knife and fork at your designated place. Are you going to put up with the interest of the rest of the workforce as you go through this ritual, or will you decide you really don't need that biscuit?

You don't necessarily have to use the plate, knife and fork, but you do need to set them out.

4. When Eating, Do Only That

Don't watch television, read or knit. You are going to dine rather than shovel. Make eating an event. Maybe you could put your drink of water or wine in a beautiful glass. You could use doilies to make the meal special. Lay the table with your finest china. Eat slowly. Savour every mouthful.

Food is simply fuel for the body, just as petrol is fuel for your car. You wouldn't take your car to the garage and ask for it to be filled up with petrol while you drive through. You would:

1. Stop the car (lay the table).
2. Get it ready to receive the fuel it needs by taking off the petrol cap (sit down at the table and contemplate what the food will taste like).
3. Fill the car with petrol at the speed it needs to receive it (eat slowly and gracefully).

Many years ago, my brother gave me a great piece of advice. I used to pig out on Victoria plums when they were in season. I would walk into town each morning (convincing myself that the walk would burn off any calories I consumed - after all, plums don't contain many calories, do they?). I would buy a pound of plums, every morning, all through the season. I would then get annoyed if anyone asked for one. I would rather they had told me in advance that they were likely to want one so I could have bought a pound and a half (greedy pig syndrome).

One day, my brother advised me to go to town the following morning and search until I found the perfect plum - just one plum, but a perfect one. Then I was to take it home, polish it, and put it on a beautiful plate with a doily. I should then look at it for 20 minutes and imagine what it would taste like when I eventually ate it. By this time I was drooling at the thought of it. It would be the best plum I had ever tasted. It would be far more enjoyable than the pound of plums. Do you know what? He was right.

I used to meet up with a group of friends each Friday afternoon to have lunch in a restaurant. Jane, one of these friends (name changed to protect the guilty!), used her lunch hour from work for this pleasure. She had been seeing me in a professional capacity to learn how to lose some excess weight.

One particular day, Jane arrived late and ordered some soup and a roll. When the food arrived she began to bolt it down. I asked her why she was doing this and she replied, 'I am late and won't be able to finish it by the time I have to be back at work.' I suggested to her that she slow down, as she would feel full within 20 minutes whether all the food was consumed or just some of it. She did slow down, and managed to get through half the soup and half the roll before she left. Jane reported later that she had indeed felt just as satisfied as she would have done by eating all the food at a faster rate.

5. Chew Each Mouthful Thoroughly

Chew your food well, and wait until each mouthful has been swallowed before putting the next on the fork. This doesn't mean you have to put your hands behind your head or sit on them until the food is chewed and swallowed. Relax your arms and rest your hands while chewing and swallowing, then bring your hand to the plate to get the next forkful ready for consumption.

If you have food in your mouth and the next mouthful is ready on your fork, what are you likely to do with the food in your mouth? You are likely to swallow it quickly to get the next forkful in. Resting your hands between each mouthful will enable you to slow down the eating process and give yourself time to savour the taste - and also to remember to chew thoroughly before swallowing.

6. Dine ... Don't Shovel

Always leave the table feeling you could have eaten a little more. I don't mean leave the table starving with hunger. Suppose you had eaten your dinner and you knew you still had room for a pudding. Now that you are no longer telling yourself you must not have pudding, you will probably be quite happy to put it away for later.

Some of your early conditioning may have been to always clear your plate, no matter whether your body needed it or not. You got used to eating until you felt bloated. Have you ever eaten so much, say at Christmas dinner, that the only thing you wanted to do afterwards was to lie down? Someone always suggests at this time that you all go out for a walk, don't they? They did at my house. I called the offender's bluff once and the expression on his face was a picture. He had eaten far more than I had, and I felt as though I was going to burst. Goodness knows what *he* must have felt like.

If you get used to leaving the table before you get to this state, you will find that a few minutes after leaving the table, that slightly empty feeling turns to energy. The full-up signal has clicked in. If you get into the habit of doing this, you will soon find it becomes automatic and you can begin to enjoy a light, energetic feeling rather than that full-to-bursting feeling.

7. Feel Pride, Not Guilt, When Disposing of Unwanted Food

It is far more of a waste to put the food into your body when your body doesn't need it and will turn it to fat. It is better to put it in the bin. Bins don't have heart attacks; people do. All you have been guilty of is misjudging how hungry you were, and you are liable to do this quite often as you first put this programme into effect. We all get into the habit of putting a certain amount of food onto the plate instead of judging how much we actually need.

I prefer to consume a small amount, then ask myself 'Do I need any more?' If I do, I then put another small portion in my mouth and ask the same question. I continue in this vein until I get the answer, 'No, your body has enough fuel for the time being.' I then stop eating.

If you are eating in a restaurant, you have paid for the meal whether you eat one teaspoon of each thing on your plate or the whole thing. If you have enjoyed the food you have eaten, it is not necessary to finish it just because you have paid for it. Maybe you imagine the waiter or the chef will feel rejected? Believe me, it is better to have savoured and truly enjoyed what you have eaten than to come away remembering nothing but how uncomfortably full the meal left you feeling.

You may be invited to dine at a friend's house - but beware if that friend is overweight. He or she may try to press you to eat more than you need, especially if this person knows you are trying to do something about your weight. Friends may not even realize they are doing this (as it may be subconscious), but they would feel better if you failed just as they are failing. If this happens to you, perhaps you should present them with a copy of this book!

The old programming may be taking effect if you feel guilty at wasting food. Maybe your mother frowned on waste, or led you to believe you were being a 'good girl' or 'good boy' by eating up all the food on your plate. Some mothers find it difficult to show love by cuddling or telling their child that he or she is loved. If, for example, a mother never experienced this affection from her own mother, then she will probably be uncomfortable showing her feelings in this way. She then finds other ways to show love, such as buying things for her children doing everything for them or feeding them. A mother who behaves in this way is usually overweight and will tend to have an overweight child, as she needs her child to eat all the food she offers in order to feel that her expression of love is accepted.

8. Never Go Food Shopping When You Are Hungry

When you stick to this rule, the only thing that will get fat is your purse or wallet. If you are hungry when you shop, you will tend to impulse-buy and purchase more than you either want or need. You will see things you fancy, and into the shopping trolley they'll go. You have no chance of eating them all at once (and probably no intention of doing so), but because these things are in the house you will tend to eat them even when you are not hungry. Always eat something like a piece of fruit or your breakfast before you shop, or only shop after a meal.

9. Find a Picture of Yourself as You Wish to Be

Find a photograph, if you have one, of yourself at the ideal body shape and weight. Alternatively, you could cut out a picture from a clothing catalogue. Stick this on the refrigerator, larder, biscuit tin, or whatever contains your greatest temptation, and make a point of looking many times a day at this image of what you will be.

I believe some slimming clubs used to advise slimmers to stick a picture of a pig in these places, but doing this gives you the wrong message. It says, 'If I eat this food I will look like a pig.' This message is telling you that you must not have this particular type of food, and thereby increases your desire for it. By having a picture of you as you *wish* to be, you give yourself an entirely different *positive* message: 'I would rather look like this picture than have this type of food.' Again, you are giving yourself choices.

10. Visualize Yourself as the Right Body Weight Now

Imagine people admiring your figure. Imagine what you would look like dressed in different outfits when you have acquired this shape. In this way you are beginning a process of reprogramming your subconscious by repetition. (More about your subconscious 'computer' later on.)

After a time, when the photo has curled up at the edges and you have become used to it being there, you may think you'll no longer notice it and might as well remove it. This is not the case. Your subconscious continues to notice.

Perhaps this concept needs further explanation. Have you ever moved the contents of a cupboard to another place which is more convenient, only to find you repeatedly go to the original cupboard? Your subconscious had been programmed by repetition to go to the original place, just as your subconscious will notice the picture on the fridge even when it no longer *consciously* registers with you.

Always imagine yourself with the beautiful figure and shape shown on the photograph as though you possess this shape *now*. If you push it into the future (e.g. 'This is what I will look like soon'), your subconscious will do the same - we all know that tomorrow never comes.

Your subconscious mind takes things literally, in exactly the same way a computer does. A computer does not use reason or common sense. Imagine you have two clocks. One is 20 minutes fast and the other has stopped. Which one would a computer (logic) say is of more use? The one that has stopped, because at least it will be telling the right time twice a day. This is not common sense, but it is logical. In just the same way, your subconscious computer is logical, or literal - so be careful which programs you insert!

Be precise with your wording. For example, 'I will lose all the fat from my body' = anorexia.

Be precise in what you want. If you say to yourself 'I would like to be nine stone, but ten would be good. The slimming magazines say I should be eight and a half, but if I reach nine or nine and a half I will be happy,' you will confuse your subconscious computer and it will have no clear idea of what weight you really want to be. Eight-and-a-half, nine, nine-and-a-half or ten stone? Be precise, and your subconscious will do the rest.

Chapter Four

Tricks Your Mind Plays

Alter Your Self-image

Have you noticed that people who have been on crash diets, even though they have temporarily lost a lot of weight, continue to walk and hold themselves as though they are still fat? This is because they have not altered their self-image.

Clients who come to my consulting rooms to learn to lose weight walk and move as though they are slim and sylph-like long before they have attained the ideal body weight - simply because they have begun the process of reprogramming their subconscious computer. They begin *seeing* themselves as slim and healthy, ready for when they really are. They report that they feel surprised when they catch sight of themselves in a shop window, as they have forgotten how much fat they are still carrying. Their self-image has definitely changed.

FIRST COMES THE MIND CHANGE, THEN THE BODY CHANGE - IT ONLY WORKS IN THIS WAY

Someone once said, 'When imagination (subconscious processes) and will power (conscious mind) are at war, imagination always wins the day.'

Imagine, for instance, you were asked to walk along a plank of wood that was placed on the ground. The plank is 9 inches wide and 12 feet in length. You would have no problem, would you? But imagine being asked to walk across that same plank of wood if it had been placed between two tower blocks 100 feet above ground level. See how powerful your imagination is now! You would almost certainly wobble and fall off, simply because that is what you *imagine* will happen. It is a self-fulfilling prophecy. 'When imagination and will-power are at war ...'

Slow but Steady

It is far better to lose weight slowly and steadily. Many people get disheartened if the weight appears to be coming off too slowly. Yet if you lose only one pound a week, this equals 52 pounds a year. Two pounds a week is 104 pounds a year, etc. You have more chance of the weight staying off if you lose it slowly, as you are re-educating your subconscious mind.

Do It for Yourself

It is important to the success of this programme that you want the change for *yourself*, rather than because your partner, boyfriend, girlfriend, etc. would prefer it if you weighed less. If you are losing weight to please someone else, what are you likely to do if you are angry with that person? More than likely, all motivation will be lost and the reaction will be to 'binge'. I'll show you how to embrace wholeheartedly the idea of a fitter you - for yourself alone.

Your Subconscious Mind Doesn't Know the Difference

Your subconscious mind cannot understand the difference between a real event and an imagined one. I will be explaining this concept in more detail later on in this book. It is the most important aspect of this book, and can change your life for the better in so many ways, once it is fully understood.

Keep a Record

So now you know the basics of changing your eating habits and losing weight. Now let's make it PERMANENT.

The charts on pages 75 to 83 are for you to record everything you consume in the next three weeks. Please note, these are *not* diet sheets.

Sometimes people forget that they have eaten and, when a meal time comes along, eat again, even when they are not particularly hungry. An example would be that, having eaten breakfast at 8.30 a.m., you then feel peckish and have a sandwich at 11. You then forget about the sandwich and, at 12.30, think to yourself, 'Hey, it's lunchtime. I had better eat something.' At the end of the day, when thinking back to what you have consumed, you have forgotten the sandwich completely. You may do this several times a week and then wonder why the weight is not budging - as, after all, you haven't eaten much, have you? By keeping the chart for the next three weeks you will be reminded of everything you have eaten - and you are more likely to eat only when you are hungry.

It is important to get into the habit of eating only when your body needs it rather than because it is a regular meal time. Get back in touch with your body clock.

Chapter Five

Your Conscious Mind and Your Subconscious Mind

- *Conscious Mind = Logic and Reason*
- *Subconscious Mind = Autonomic Nervous System (Your Survival Instinct)*

Just as you need to know the three 'rules' of eating slowly, chewing thoroughly and noticing the taste of everything, as well as why these 'rules' are important, now you need to know a little of how the mind works to enable your ideal body weight and shape to become permanent. You will also discover, by the end of this chapter, why you have had such difficulty previously, and how to make this difficulty a thing of the past.

You have two distinctly different parts of your mind: the conscious mind and the subconscious mind.

Your Conscious Mind

The conscious part of your mind is the part you are using now. It uses logic, intelligence, common sense and reason. It works things out based on past experience. This is its function. We are taught how to use this part of the mind by teachers, parents, etc. If your problem of too much weight was in this part of your mind, then giving yourself a good talking to would solve the problem. You would simply decide you needed less food and wanted to be a certain size and shape. You would consume less and achieve your goal. If it had anything to do with will-power, you would be able to stick to that decision and lose the weight and keep it off. Think about it! You probably have lots of will-power in other areas of your life. The problem is not within the *conscious* part of your mind, but within the *subconscious*.

Your Subconscious Mind

The subconscious part of the mind is very different from the conscious. The subconscious is the autonomic nervous system. It makes you blush, cough, sweat, sneeze. It keeps your heart beating, your lungs functioning. It replaces chemicals that have been depleted. It is in charge of cell regeneration. It is dreams, day-dreams, imagination, habits, emotions. All the things you do automatically are located in the subconscious. Your appetite, your metabolic rate, your cravings and desires are also in this part of the mind.

The subconscious is not a little part of the brain tucked at the back of your head somewhere, as most people believe. It is about ten-elevenths of your brain (I'd love to know who measures these things, but this is the accepted ratio in psychology). Most people know how to use only one-eleventh of the capacity of their mind. Einstein, on a good day, accepted he used about three-elevenths. Here's the good news: you are about to learn how to use *all* of your mind.

Think of your subconscious as a huge computer. If you program a computer to recognize that two and two equal five, it will continue to generate this, no matter how much you shouted at it with your conscious mind, 'Hey! I want that to be four now!'

In just the same way, your subconscious computer has a program of you, as you are now. It has information on your size, height, shape, weight, whether or not you are a smoker, nail-biter, etc., and it thinks this is right as, after all, you are surviving.

Your subconscious is there to ensure your survival. It cares not a jot about happiness or achievement. It puts survival first. If survival is not threatened it encourages the positive emotions. So, no matter how much you shout at it with your conscious mind, 'Hey! I want to be a different shape, weight and size!', it will continue to reinstate the original program.

Can you now see why you have been having such difficulty sticking to that diet? You have been fighting your subconscious survival instinct.

Wouldn't It Make More Sense to Reprogram the Computer?

Your subconscious mind knows how to make changes. Once your internal 'computer' has accepted a new program of a fitter, healthier you, it *has* to work with this program. It does not have a choice it has to use all it's resources to create the new program. It will speed up your metabolic rate. It will give you more energy. You will lose the desire for sweet, sugary things. You might think of eating something sweet, but your subconscious will tell you that it would be just too sickly. The thought of eating something oily or greasy will also become slightly repulsive to you, as you will much prefer clean, crisp tastes in your mouth.

Right, so let's get reprogramming!

Chapter Six

The Power of Self-hypnosis

You are now going to learn how easy it is going to be to put whatever you wish into your subconscious computer. I am going to teach you how to use self-hypnosis, as it is the easiest and most efficient way of accessing and reprogramming this subconscious computer of yours.

Hypnosis Is a Natural State

First let me dispel a few of the myths about hypnosis, as I want you to be as comfortable as you can be with inducing hypnosis for yourself.

Hypnosis needs, and is, only a state of relaxation. It is not some magical state. Neither is it devil worship or brain-washing. Swinging watches or staring eyes play no part. It is not taking over someone's will.

All Hypnosis Is Self-hypnosis

The only person I have ever hypnotized is myself, and the same goes for any hypnotherapist. Yes, even the stage hypnotists. (I will explain how they do what they do later.) It is logical when you think about it. If a hypnotherapist had the power to take over someone's will by using hypnosis, wouldn't everyone want to train as a hypnotherapist?

You already go into self-hypnosis many times a day, but may not realize you have this skill. Hypnosis is a perfectly natural state of relaxation. Everyone is in hypnosis at least twice every day of their lives, and probably many more times. The most easily recognizable times are just before falling asleep and just after waking up in the morning. Picture the scene. You are in bed. The alarm rings and you would give your right arm for five more minutes. You know you are capable of getting up, but can't be bothered. If someone speaks to you, you hear them, but are too relaxed and sleepy to take much notice. This lethargic state is hypnosis. Nothing more, nothing less.

If you want to amaze your friends with your brilliance, you can use two very psychological-sounding names for this everyday hypnotic state: hypnopompic and hypnogogic. The hypnopompic state is just after waking up; the hypnogogic state is just before falling asleep.

Another recognizable time of being in a hypnotic state is what you would probably describe as day-dreaming, or meditating. These are states of hypnosis. Imagine you have been driving for a long period of time and you ask yourself, 'Where have the last 10 miles gone? I don't remember passing the usual landmarks.' You have been driving in a hypnotic state. It is quite safe, as your subconscious knows how to drive.

Have you ever become so engrossed in a book or a television programme that you have been unaware of whatever was going on in the room around you? This again is a light state of hypnosis.

Because it is impossible for me to come to you just as you are falling asleep, waking up, reading, watching TV or walking the dog, I am going to teach you how to hypnotize yourself. It is really easy to do. You could even hypnotize someone else if you were to read them the contents of the telephone book in a boring voice for long enough. It's called 'boring them into hypnosis' in the profession.

No One Can Take Over Your Will

In my consulting rooms, as a hypnotherapist, I have had clients who think they will go off to the planet Zod and wake up on my consulting couch as new people. I wish it were that easy. I have even had people ask me if I could hypnotize them and get them to pay all their money into my bank account. What a lovely thought! If this were possible, I would be pushing a wheelbarrow full of money to the bank every morning, and spending the winters in the Bahamas.

Think about it. If you could get this kind of power over people using hypnosis, everyone would come rushing to my academy to learn the art.

A frequent response from clients is 'I didn't go under.' I wonder what they thought was going to happen? They also say, 'I heard every word you said.' Well, there wouldn't be much point if they hadn't! One of the funniest reactions I have had was 'I could have got up and walked away if I had wanted to.' Precisely. Hypnosis does not make you lose any of your own will-power or self-control.

In other words, there is no such thing as a hypnotized feeling, any more than there is a feeling of being in a day-dream. If you are thinking to yourself, 'I am day-dreaming now,' then you must have brought yourself out of that day-dream to analyze the state.

Hopefully I have dispelled some of the myths surrounding this naturally occurring state because, when you have learned to induce this state yourself, you will have a tool that can change your life for the better in many ways.

Your Conscious and Subconscious Mind Cannot Work at the Same Time

When in a state of self-hypnosis your subconscious mind is to the fore. Or, in other words, you have turned on your subconscious computer.

It's important to understand that your subconscious and conscious mind cannot work together. Either one is working, or the other, but not both.

Everything you have ever done, thought, learned, tasted, or felt is stored in your subconscious mind. It is like a vast library.

Imagine you meet someone familiar but you cannot remember his name. Your subconscious immediately goes into action by searching through its memory banks to find the name. It finds it, but cannot get it through to conscious awareness because you are so busy using the conscious part of your mind 'trying to remember'. What happens when you stop 'trying'? Your subconscious can now use its filter system to push it through to your conscious awareness. You startle everyone by leaping up and shouting 'It's Roger' at 2 o'clock in the morning. The answer usually comes in the early hours as you are very relaxed (in hypnosis) and are, therefore, not using the conscious, analytical, part of your mind, and so allowing the subconscious free rein.

Some of the following chapters will show you how to access your subconscious computer to insert whatever program you choose, using the process of self-hypnosis. For the purposes of this book you will be shown how to insert a program of yourself at your ideal body weight. But once you have mastered the self-hypnosis technique, you can use it for many different purposes, such as to stop smoking, build self-confidence, pass exams or your driving test, become a better sportsperson, increase your wealth, or anything else you may choose. There are no limits except the limits in your belief system. But in this book we will concentrate on weight control.

I said earlier that the subconscious computer is programmed by using repetition. Can you see why it is better for you to learn how to hypnotize yourself? You can then use the repetitive process at your leisure.

I also said earlier that no one can be made to do anything against their will by a hypnotherapist or hypnotist, and yet I expect you have seen stage hypnotists doing just this. Now, as promised, I will explain.

Any stage hypnotist will always ask for volunteers from the audience. You will never see a stage hypnotist dragging someone onto the stage. Anyone volunteering to take part in a stage show will fit into one of two character types. A person of the first type will have an extrovert nature - probably someone who has seen a stage show before and knows what to expect. He will want to be the star of the show, make a fool of himself, yet take no responsibility for this. He can blame it all on the hypnotist, yet nothing the hypnotist asks him to do can be against his will. He will *want* to perform the tasks requested of him.

The other type of volunteer will likely be someone who just wants to prove to the audience and the hypnotist that his mind is the stronger. He will be determined not to allow the hypnotist to hypnotize him. The hypnotist knows, of course, he is unable to hypnotize anybody against their will. Guess which volunteer he sends back to the seats? You've guessed it. The second one, of course.

So, how does he hypnotize someone when I said all hypnosis is self-hypnosis?

The stage hypnotist will line up the volunteers so each one can see the others in the line. The first volunteer will either be someone who has been to a stage show before, or even someone (if the hypnotist is lucky) the hypnotist has helped into the state before. If there is no one available who fits this category, the hypnotist will have brought someone with him who knows the ropes. He will then go through a seemingly magical ritual, maybe clicking his fingers and shouting 'sleep'. (He could shout 'fish fingers'. It would still work.) The first volunteer will go into a trance, as it is his belief that this is what will occur. It is not the hypnotist who has hypnotized the volunteer. It is the belief of the volunteer that has enabled hypnosis to occur.

Let us go back to that line of volunteers. The second person in the line has seen what happened to the first one when the hypnotist clicked his fingers. What do you suppose he is thinking? And what do you suppose will happen to this volunteer when the hypnotist clicks his fingers and shouts 'sleep' at him? Is it the hypnotist who has hypnotized the volunteer, or is it the belief of the volunteer that has induced the hypnotic trance?

Think about number 12 in the line of volunteers. What do you think will happen to this one on the click of the hypnotist's fingers? I think you get the point.

I know it must seem as if I am going on at length about hypnosis, but it is of paramount importance that you fully understand the hypnotic state, and that you feel comfortable with it. It is about to change your life for the better. This knowledge will put you fully in control of yourself and your future happiness and achievements in life. It can help you to achieve all that you want to achieve. It will certainly enable you to achieve your perfect body weight for the rest of your life.

Some people will buy a computer only to find they don't have the patience to go through the manual. They have a go, make a few mistakes, and put it away. Another person might learn the basics, such as writing letters and playing games, but never bother to explore everything the computer can do. Yet another will buy that computer and spend time learning everything it will do. By devoting time and effort to understanding all the things the computer can do for him, this person will greatly enhance his life. So it is with learning about and using self-hypnosis.

You could read this book and decide it is taking too much of your time and go on yet another diet. You could use self-hypnosis only for weight control. Or you could learn this valuable technique and get control of many areas of your life. I wonder which it will be? It's up to you.

Chapter Seven

Reprogramming Your Subconscious Computer

You are now almost ready to begin to put all you have learned thus far into practice. You can now adapt your eating habits to use the three 'rules' of eating slowly, chewing thoroughly and noticing the taste of everything you put into your mouth. This will quickly become habitual, or automatic, and you should lose weight steadily. There are just a few more things you need to understand.

When you are dreaming, or day-dreaming, you are utilizing your subconscious.

Think of when you dream. Your dreams can seem very logical and real at the time you are dreaming them, but if someone were to rouse you during that dream, your conscious, logical mind would click in and sort out the fantasy from the reality. You would be likely to think, 'Hey! That seemed so real, but it was ridiculous.'

Suppose you were dreaming of a duck walking by with red wellington boots on, taking snapshots of dragons. It would all make sense and seem quite plausible while you were having the dream, but what happens when you wake - assuming you remember the details contained within the dream? As your conscious, analytical mind sorts out reality from fantasy you recognize that ducks have webbed feet so couldn't possibly walk with wellington boots on. And how could it take photographs of dragons when ducks have wings, not hands, and dragons do not exist?

When you use the same process to imagine yourself to be the ideal body weight now, your subconscious has no way of knowing this is not fact. If you then make it repetitive (by using self-hypnosis), your subconscious accepts it totally as a program and has no choice but to instigate this program. This program of you at a perfect body weight for your height is much stronger in your subconscious than in your conscious mind, and so cannot be analysed away. Your subconscious will then use all its resources to sustain this program.

You will find you automatically feel 'full up' when you've eaten far less than is usual. You will also find you no longer fancy sweet, sugary things, or oily, greasy foods. In fact, the thought of eating this type of food may even make you feel nauseous. You will prefer a nice, clean, fresh taste in your mouth.

Your dreams come from the subconscious part of the mind and, if you remember, your conscious and subconscious mind cannot work at the same time. When you dream, your subconscious mind does not analyse the situation, but accepts it as reality. Can you see now why my clients walk and move as though they were already their ideal body weight? The subconscious computer has the program of them this way, and this is their reality.

This is the premise you are going to use to reprogram your subconscious computer. Have you ever heard a very slim person say, 'I can eat whatever I like and never gain an ounce'? This is their reality, or program.

When you imagine yourself as a fitter, healthier, slimmer you, while using self-hypnosis (accessing the computer), your subconscious does not know this is fantasy at this moment in time, and it will have to use its resources to create the image you are programming into the computer. In other words, you are bypassing your conscious, logical mind and going straight to your subconscious mind - which just *accepts.*

Using Imagination to Heal

Self-hypnois allows you to use one aspect of your subconscious (imagination) to access another aspect (the ability to heal).

The subconscious part of your mind knows how to heal your body. It knows which chemicals are needed in any part of your body at any given time. For example, it will increase adrenaline whenever you are in a fear situation, to enable you to fight or run away. It will bring white corpuscles to the area of infection, to fight it off. It processes food and turns it into energy. This, the autonomic nervous system, is the aspect of your subconscious that is activated by using self-hypnosis (imagination).

The following chapters will give scripts that you can put onto a cassette to use at your leisure, and instruction on learning self-hypnosis for times when it may be inconvenient to use a cassette player. There is of course a CD with this book, but you may prefer to make your own tape or to adapt this one to suit yourself.

The sentences in these scripts may seem unlikely to work while you are reading - but this is the work of your conscious, analytical mind. Your subconscious will accept them totally. Trust it and it will work for you. Just be in a receptive mode while listening to them or using self-hypnosis.

If you are telling yourself, 'This will not work for me', your subconscious will accept this negative statement and you will be sabotaging your chance of success. Many people know that positive thinking works, but do not understand why. You do.

An extension of hypnosis is sleep, so don't worry about not being able to bring yourself out of hypnosis. The worst that can happen is that you will fall asleep during the playing of the CD and wake up naturally when you've rested. You are quite likely to do this anyway, especially when you have played the recording a few times and have become familiar with what is coming next. This *is* hypnosis: your conscious mind will have drifted off while your subconscious takes in the suggestions, without effort from your conscious mind. It doesn't really matter whether you sleep or listen more actively, the effect will be the same.

Chapter Eight

Self-hypnosis Scripts

Induction

[*I recommend that you 'speak' this script, exactly as it is written, and as if you were giving instruction to someone else who will be playing the cassette or disc you are about to record.*]
  [*Begin as follows, the dots represent pauses:*]

I assume that you are sitting comfortably, or lying down. Allow your eyes to gently close and let the everyday world just fade away, giving your thoughts time to become still and quiet ...

The easiest way to do this is to focus inwards into your breathing ... Gentle, easy breathing ... Notice the gentle rise and fall of your chest with each breath ... Notice the feel of the breathing in your throat and your nose ... Notice the gentle sound of your breathing.

Just accept, for the next little while, that this is your time to relax ... with no demands on you ... no expectations of you ... no marks out of ten for achievement ... There is nothing whatsoever for you to do except to enjoy the feelings that come ... Feelings of peacefulness ... calmness ... and tranquillity ...

During this period of relaxation, if anything should need your urgent attention, you will just get up and deal with it, but whilst you can remain relaxed, I'd like you to do just that ...

Each gentle breath is relaxing you deeper and deeper and deeper still ... gently breathing away tension ... gently breathing away stress ... breathing in calmness ... breathing out tension ... breathing in tranquillity ... breathing out stress ...

Every nerve ... every muscle ... every cell in your body is relaxing deeper ... and deeper ... and deeper still ... A sort of 'letting-go' feeling, as though you are sinking down into the bed or chair beneath you ...

In a moment I will ask you to take three, very slow, very deep breaths ... and when I ask you to take those three, very slow, very deep breaths, I will ask you to gently hold each breath ... and when

you let the breath go, just think to yourself the word 'relaaaaaaax'...
Now, in your own time, just take those three very slow, very deep
breaths.

[*Leave yourself plenty of time for the three breaths to be taken, then
carry on with your tape recording, saying:*]

With every breath that you take ... and with every word that I speak
... relaxing deeper ... and deeper ... and deeper still ...
Nothing bothers you ... nothing disturbs you ... You just couldn't
care less ...
When you have completed these three, slow, deep breaths ... allow
your breathing to settle to whatever is normal for you ... and with
every breath that you take ... and with every word that I speak ... you
are relaxing deeper ... and deeper ... and deeper still.
Focus your awareness now on the top of your head ... Just think of
your scalp ... where tension begins ... Let your scalp relax ... and your
forehead ... Let them relax now ... Feel all those tiny little frown lines
smoothing out ... and just disappearing ... The space between your
eyebrows seems to widen as you let go ... completely ...
Feel your eyes relaxing now ... All those tiny little nerves ... all those
tiny muscles surrounding your eyes ... all relaxed and resting ... perfectly at ease ... as you drift deeper ... and deeper ... and deeper still ...
With every breath that you take ... and with every word that I speak ...
you are drifting deeper ... and deeper ... and deeper still ... sinking or
floating ... drifting and dreaming ...
Allow your cheeks to relax now ... Your teeth unclench ... your ton-
gue is relaxed ... your jaw is relaxed ... they are all limp and relaxed ...
Enjoy this lovely, lazy feeling as you let yourself go completely ...
Imagine a warm glow of relaxation flowing through your entire
body ... spreading out to every nerve ending ... wave after wave of
relaxation flowing down from the top of your head, right down to
your toes ...
Let that warm glow of relaxation flow down into your neck and
shoulders now ... and feel those nerves and muscles in your neck
and shoulders just sag and go limp ... just like a rag doll ... all limp,
relaxed and resting ... as though your muscles are made of cotton
wool ...
And allow your arms to relax ... your forearms, and elbows, wrists,

hands, fingers and thumbs ... all relaxed and resting ... perfectly at ease ... Your fingers soften and go limp ...

A soft warmth flows through your body now ... spreading out to every nerve ending ... beautifully relaxed ... perfectly at ease as you drift deeper ... and deeper ... and deeper still ... And with every breath you take ... and with every word that I speak ... drifting ... deeper ... and deeper ... and deeper still ... drifting and floating ... lazily dreaming ...

Now focus your awareness on your chest ... Your breathing is healthy, natural, effortless, at peace, at rest ...

Focus on your spine, your abdomen and right down to your waist ... From the top of your head, right down to your waist ... All relaxed and resting ... perfectly at ease ... And nothing bothers you ... and nothing concerns you ... You just couldn't care less ... as that warm soothing feeling of relaxation spreads through your entire body ... And you just let go completely ...

And no matter how deeply you relax, you will be able to hear my voice at some level ... so there is no need to try to listen to my voice ...

Your mind follows your body ... Your mind relaxes ... drifting and dreaming ... wonderfully relaxed and peaceful ...

That warm glow of relaxation spreads now through your hips and your tummy muscles, and your buttocks, and the muscles below your tummy ... all relaxed and resting ... perfectly at ease ... all tension is just draining away ... like water draining out of a bath ... as you drift deeper ... and deeper ... and deeper still ... all relaxed and resting ...

That same warmth is now spreading down your thighs ... and your knees ... and your calves and shins ... to your ankles, heels, feet and toes ...

From the top of your head right down to your toes ... as though you are wrapped in a soft warm blanket of relaxation ... all warm and snug and cosy ... perfectly at ease ... as you drift deeper ... and deeper ... and deeper still ... Relax and let go completely ... giving yourself permission to rest ... to relax ... to utterly let go ...

[Continue with]
Deepening

Notice how relaxed you have become ...

If you were asked to lift your legs now, it would be just too much effort, as they are so relaxed and comfortable just where they are ...

If you were asked to raise your head, it would be just too much bother, as it is so wonderfully relaxed just as it is ...

And this awareness takes you deeper ... and deeper into relaxation ... becoming even more relaxed ... even more peaceful ...

And now to deepen that state ... and to become even more relaxed ... even more peaceful ... imagine you are standing at the top of a hill on a perfect summer's afternoon ... Just standing at the top of that hill without a care in the world ... no pressure of time ... no demands on you.

Looking down a long winding path, leading down into a valley ... maybe you can see into the valley from the top of the hill ... This is a very peaceful, tranquil place with nobody about for miles and miles ... your own secret place ... your own secret paradise ...

Notice a stream winding through the valley ... sunlight glinting on the crystal-clear water of the stream ... like a silver ribbon winding through the valley ...

In a moment I am going to count from ten, down ... down to zero ... and as I count from ten, down to zero, with each number I count you can relax twenty times deeper ... becoming twenty times more relaxed ... and twenty times more peaceful than you were at the number before ...

TEN ... Feel the warmth of the sun on your skin ... soothing, calming and

relaxing ...

NINE ... Feel a warm breeze on your face and your body ...

EIGHT ... Hear the sound of your footsteps on the path ... and feel the muscles in your legs as you stroll lazily down the path ...

SEVEN ... Hear the birds chattering in the trees ... the warm breeze rustling the leaves of the trees ...

SIX ... Maybe there is a stile here ... you can climb gently over the stile and continue to stroll gently down the path ...

FIVE ... Halfway there now ... Turn slightly ... Look back at the top of the hill ... It's all hazy now ... The everyday world and all its problems just fading away as you stroll deeper and deeper into that inner world ...

FOUR ... Becoming weightless now ... all weight has drained away and you are floating and drifting, quite safely, just two inches above the path ... floating and drifting ...

THREE ... Hear the lazy droning sound of the insects, buzzing in the warm sunshine ... Smell that distinctive smell of new-cut grass all around you ...

TWO ... Perhaps you can see some animals, maybe ... Rabbits hopping across the fields ... A squirrel running up a tree ...

ONE ... Nearly there now ... Maybe you can already hear the sound of trickling water in the stream ...

ZERO ... Right down in the valley now, feeling safe, secure and peaceful ...

[*Continue with*]
Positive Suggestions and Imagery

Stroll over the grass now toward the stream ... Just absorbing all the calmness ... all the peacefulness of this place ... Your secret place ...

Notice a full-length mirror, there on the grass ...

[*Make your voice slowly become a little more excited*]

As you approach the mirror, you see an image of yourself at the perfect weight for your height, reflected in that mirror ... This is the real you ... with not an ounce of excess fat anywhere ... Your muscles are firm and strong ... your skin is firm and smooth ... You are at the perfect body weight for your height ...

Looking stunning ...

That image of you is perhaps dressed in the height of fashion, or with an outfit from a top couturier ... See how good it looks ... How well the clothes fit ...

Now, just like Alice Through the Looking Glass, step into that mirror ... Step into that image of the real you ... Reclaim it ... Feel what it is like ... This is the you, *at the perfect body weight for your height* ...

Now, step right through the mirror ... bringing that image with you ... This image is now you ...

Run your hands down your body ... and feel how good you feel ... how firm and strong your muscles are ... Feel your gentle curves ... Your stomach - flat and tight, like an ironing board ... Notice how much more energy you now have ... Notice how good you feel ... The real you ...

Walk over to the stream now ... Notice how much lighter you feel as you walk across the grass to the stream ... You have a bounce in your step ... a spring in your heels ...

As you stand looking into the crystal-clear water of the stream, notice that your mouth has become incredibly dry ... as though the heat of the sun has dried up all the moisture in your mouth ... Your lips feel dry and cracked ... your mouth hot and dry ... your throat coarse and scratchy ... getting drier and drier ... getting warmer and warmer ... hotter and hotter - thirstier and thirstier ...

Notice there, beside that healing stream, a beautiful cut-crystal glass ... Fill the glass from the healing water of the stream ... Notice the condensation running down the outside of the glass ... Notice the sunlight glistening on the crystal-clear cold water in the glass ... Feel the fresh coldness as the water goes into your mouth ... and feel the soothing freshness in your throat ... As you swallow the water, notice a tingle of energy flowing through your body ...

[*Increase the energy in your voice now, making it more excited, and speaking a little more quickly. You won't bring yourself out of hypnosis.*]

You are drinking liquid energy ... feeling that energy flowing out to every nerve ending, from the top of your head, right down to your toes ... In astonishment you drink from the glass again ... Again, feel that buzz of energy coursing through your body ... making you feel so vitally alive ... You are laughing inside ... knowing you could run a hundred miles effortlessly ... knowing you could leap that stream in one bound ...

You begin to run alongside the stream ... laughing ... It is so effortless ... You run up the hill, and down the other side ... Leaping that stream ...

As you have imagined this, so shall it be ... This is now fixed firmly in the subconscious of your mind ... and every time you drink water ... whether it is from a bottle or a tap ...
whether it is made into a hot drink or a cold drink, you will feel that energy coursing through your body ... healing, restoring, revitalizing, re-energizing ... making you feel so alive ... and ...

In the days and weeks ahead, any time you drink water you will find, to your delight, that a tingle of energy buzzes through your body, filling you with energy and vitality. In the days and weeks ahead you will find, to your pleasure, that the desire to eat sweet sugary foods has drifted away, easily, naturally, and effortlessly. You will find that the need for oily, greasy foods has also just disappeared and that you actually enjoy the feel and taste of clean, cool, fresh water in your mouth ... You will find you prefer clean, crisp tastes rather than the foods you used to eat, and you will find your energy and vitality increasing noticeably day by day.

[*As you commence the 'waking-up' procedures on your recording, you should speak more quietly, calmly and in a gentler tone.*]

Waking Up

Visualize a flight of steps now ... There are five steps and you are standing at the bottom looking up ... Beside the steps is a very large white, soft, fluffy towel being warmed by the sun ...

If you are playing this at bedtime, and you are ready to go to sleep, you can now imagine yourself snuggling down on that soft, fluffy, towel and you can drift off into a deep refreshing sleep, confident in the knowledge that you will awaken in the morning feeling refreshed, re-energized, revitalized and ready to enjoy the new day to the full.

But if it is now time for you to arise and enjoy the rest of this beautiful day then, in a moment, I will count from one to five as you climb up those five steps, and each step you climb will make you more alert and aware. And, on the count of five, you will simply open your eyes and awake, refreshed, restored and feeling wonderful ... You'll feel a real spring in your step, and a bounce in your heel. You will feel happy, light-hearted, confident and carefree. It will be such a wonderful feeling.

If it is now time for you to sleep, reach over and turn off your tape recorder or CD player, snuggle down and drift into a deep, restful sleep ...

[*Pause here for a few moments to allow time for the tape recorder to be turned off. Then continue to record as follows:*]

If it is now time to get up and enjoy the rest of this beautiful day, listen as I count from one up to five and imagine that you are climbing those stairs and, on the count of five, you will open your eyes and realize just how good you feel ... better than you have felt for days, for weeks, for months, or even years.

ONE ... Feeling brighter now.

TWO ... Brighter still.

THREE ... A bubble of joy inside you getting bigger and bigger.

FOUR ... Becoming aware of the room around you ... and

FIVE ... Wide awake and feeling wonderful and looking forward to playing this recording again soon.

Chapter Nine

Using the CD orYour Own Cassette

Now that the tape is complete, there is only one more thing for you to do to enable you to achieve the perfect body weight for your height: you *must* listen to it or the CD that came with this book twice a day for about a month. You should organize your life so that you look forward to regularly setting aside time for yourself to enjoy the relaxation and to enjoy the recording. Tell yourself you are worth it. This is your treat and you deserve it. At the end of the month you will have established a program that will last for the rest of your life.

As you use the recording on a regular basis you will develop the art of visualization. You can use this skill, without self-hypnosis, any time throughout the day, even with your eyes wide open. All you will need to do is to take three slow deep breaths and think to yourself the word 'relaaaax'. You will immediately feel yourself becoming calm and relaxed. This will happen when you have played the tape or the pre-recorded CD a few times, as you will have programmed this in.

If at present you have a favourite outfit that no longer fits you since you have put weight on, I suggest you hang it up somewhere where you will see it often. At every opportunity, imagine yourself wearing that outfit.

Visualize the real you inside your body. Imagine your bone structure supporting firm muscles, flesh and skin. Run your hands down your body, imagining you are wiping away the unwanted bits of you, especially the excess fat that really does not belong to you. A good time to do this is when you are having a shower. As you stand in the shower washing your body, you can imagine you are washing away the bits that are not really yours. The more often you do this, the sooner you will see results.

It will not be long before you find that, whenever you 'step into that mirror' on the recording, there will be no reason for you to 'change' as you will be seeing yourself as already fitting your desired image of yourself.

If you usually keep a glass of water on the bedside table when you go to sleep, it might be a good idea now to omit this, as you don't want to be filled with energy when you are ready to sleep.

Design for Life

You now have a program that will enable you to be your perfect body weight for the rest of your life. You will never again need to diet, and your friends will want to know how you did it. Are you going to be kind and tell them, or will you keep it a secret?

Perhaps in a few years' time you will find that you have put on a couple of pounds. If so, replay your tape a few times. Watch the unwanted pounds melt away!

This process can easily be adapted to improve many other areas in your life. We'll take a look at how in Chapter 12.

Chapter Ten

Fighting Resistance

A small number of people may find that, even though they stick rigidly to the suggestions in this book, the pounds still refuse to budge. We are talking about a *very* small percentage here. These are the people who are anorexic, bulimic or very obese. But help is at hand.

I mentioned earlier that there are two ways in which things pass between the conscious and subconscious mind. The first is by repetition. The following example will illustrate the second way.

Repressed Memory

If something happens to you at any time in your life that is too traumatic for you to handle, your subconscious protects you by blocking all memory of the incident. When a traumatic incident occurs in an adult's life, this blocking process is referred to as 'amnesia'. But if it happens in childhood, it is known as 'repression'. Children repress memories of traumatic events far more than adults do, simply because children have fewer resources with which to deal with overwhelming emotion.

Every repressed memory *will* throw up symptoms later in life. One symptom *could* be an eating problem, though symptoms might also arise in other areas of life, for example as phobias, compulsive activity, or obsessional behaviour. Symptoms may manifest themselves in physical ways, such as migraine, asthma, high blood pressure or excess weight. Much depends on the psyche of the individual.

Manifestations of stress-related problems can be identified in one or more of five areas - in behavioural habits, the skin, the stomach, the head or the mind.

- *Behavioural habits: nail-biting, smoking, hair-pulling, facial tics, etc.*
- *Skin: eczema, psoriasis or frequent skin rashes*
- *Stomach: ulcers, irritable bowel syndrome, frequent stomach upsets or weight problems*

- *Head:* migraines or headaches
- *Mind:* phobias or irrational fears

Imagine for a moment that a man has a car accident. He reports that he can remember driving from his house and waking up at the hospital. But he has no recollection of the drive to the scene of the accident, the windscreen smashing into his face, or the ride in the ambulance to the hospital (even assuming he was conscious at the time). It was all too traumatic to handle, so the subconscious protects him by blocking awareness of the entire incident. To make doubly sure, the subconscious even blocks out events either side of the incident (so that, in this instance, the man's amnesia also covers the time he spent driving just before he had the accident and the journey in the ambulance to the hospital). Even though the man has no conscious memory of the accident as it happened, the man does, of course, know that he has been involved in an accident because he has the physical scars, garage bills and a damaged car to prove it.

Later in this man's life, symptoms may arise that he will not link with the car accident, as he has no conscious memory of it. He may perhaps develop a phobia of long journeys, car parks or open spaces. If the car involved in the accident was red, the man could develop a fear of the colour red. If, at the time of the accident, he was afraid that the car might burst into flames, he might develop a fear of fire.

Suppose that a mother tells her child, 'If you do that again I will kill you.' The child forgets the mothers warning and repeats the misdemeanor only then to remember what mother said. The child takes the warning literally, which results in fear and terror of being found out. This entire sequence of events is then suppressed. As a result, the child may well develop a guilt complex which might manifest itself in a variety of ways, including blushing when asked a question, feelings of rejection, low self-worth, or indeed any permutation of problems which are carried into adult life.

Suppose a client went to a hypnotherapist with a symptom of obesity. The therapist, if properly trained, would regress the patient to the beginning of the problem. In other words, the therapist would instruct the client's subconscious to reveal any underlying traumatic incident, assuring the subconscious that it is now safe to do so - whatever it was that happened to upset the child is perfectly safe for the adult to remember. The adult has many more resources available to help cope with the emotions than were available to the child when the incident occurred.

The therapist would also need to analyse and understand what protection the excess weight is giving the patient. (The subconscious *always* seeks to protect us, so the extra weight must be serving a purpose in some way.) The client, of course, would not consciously choose to carry the extra weight, but the subconscious may be functioning from outdated information.

Imagine that a child of five, during a war, is shell-shocked and not eating. She gets very thin and her parents are so concerned that they send her to hospital. When she gains a few pounds she is allowed home, but if she loses weight again she is sent back to the hospital.

Thus, a pattern is formed in the child's subconscious that she is not wanted unless she is fat. In her mind, her parents abandon her and send her to that awful place every time she loses weight. In later life, whenever she is feeling unloved, she may gain weight. She then goes on a diet. As she gets slimmer, anxiety creeps in and she is forced to put the weight back on before she can feel comfortable. Subconsciously, she fears she will be abandoned if she loses weight.

She will not be consciously aware of this process, as the childhood trauma has been repressed.

Repressed childhood memories cannot benefit from life experience - they cannot grow up, if you like - because they have been relegated to the subconscious, which is neither intelligent nor logical. The subconscious will, therefore, continue to recreate the same feelings which were experienced by the child. It does not know that the adult no longer needs to be protected from facing these underlying fears, anxieties or other feelings.

The subconscious knows how to protect, but does not always know how or when to turn the protection off. When the original trauma is raised into conscious awareness with the help of a hypno-analyst, however, it can then have logic and reason added to it. The person can now view it with her adult mind and, in the case of the woman described above, understand that she was not being abandoned. Her subconscious, therefore, no longer has a need to keep her fat. The pounds will fall off without any need to diet. She will become the person she would have been without the trauma.

This may sound complicated, but it is really quite simple. The therapist has no need to guess the probable nature of the repressed trauma, as the client's subconscious already knows what it is protecting. Using hypnosis is the easiest, fastest and most efficient way of accessing the subconscious mind.

Many of my clients start by saying that they know what is likely to have caused the problem. They then proceed to relate some traumatic incidents from their past, and identify these as the cause of their bad habits, weight gain, etc. In fact, it is highly unlikely that they are right, as consciously remembered traumas are, by definition, not repressed. We have all experienced traumatic events, but if we can remember them, then the strong emotions which accompanied them were either dealt with at the time or have been dealt with since, and so are unlikely to be causing the symptoms.

A patient, for example, might say that she can remember the incident that caused her terrible dread of spiders. 'It was when Jimmy chased me around the playground and put one down my blouse,' she might say. The therapist will then explain that this is unlikely, as the fear must have already existed or that specific incident would not have frightened her. In other words, the fear must have developed from an earlier incident.

Incidentally, in reality, a fear of spiders is rarely a true phobia. It usually develops from a child having seen an adult being afraid of a spider at a time in her life when the child was impressionable. The fear she witnessed in an adult is then carried into her own adult life. Another fear that usually has the same basis is a fear of thunderstorms.

Please accept that a trauma causing a weight problem is the exception rather than the rule. A person who is only about one or two stones overweight is unlikely to have any problem losing weight using the methods described earlier in this book. Similarly, a person who has been the ideal body weight for her height at some point in adult life is unlikely to have a problem of repressed trauma either. If you can visualize yourself at your ideal body weight without anxiety and with delight, you will have no problem making good use of the information in this book. If this is not so for you, however, then I would recommend that you seek help from a fully trained hypnoanalyst. The telephone numbers at the end of this book will assist you in finding one in your area.

Chapter Eleven

Case Histories

Janet

Janet came to my consulting rooms with a big weight problem. She was six-and-a-half stone overweight. She couldn't pick out the clothes she liked; she had to buy whatever they had in her size. Her health was at risk and she had been on various diets over the previous 30 years with no lasting success. Indeed, after every diet she actually put so much weight on that she ended up weighing more than she had before the diet.

When I took her into hypnosis and requested the subconscious regress her to the point in time when the need for the protection of excess weight first occurred, Janet found herself remembering a time when she was just 12 years old.

Her parents had had a shop, and next door was a butcher's shop. Janet used to go into the butcher's and flirt and be cheeky to the butcher boys. (You would at 12 years old, wouldn't you?) One day the butchers had had enough, so to teach her a lesson they locked her in the freezer. This was a large room with carcasses hanging from the ceiling. They knew they would let her out in a few minutes, but *she didn't*, and with the vivid imagination of a 12 year old she was imagining herself being found, weeks later, frozen solid in a block of ice.

They eventually let her out of the freezer and she ran away as fast as she could. She couldn't tell anyone, as she had been told many times by her parents not to keep bothering the butchers. She pushed the memory to the back of her mind, wishing it hadn't happened (this is known as *disavowal*), and eventually the memory disappeared from her conscious awareness (*repression*). If you had asked her about it she would have said it never happened, as she had no conscious memory of it.

Because the memory was now in the subconscious part of Janet's mind, it could not 'grow up' or have conscious logic added to it. Her subconscious had no way of knowing she wasn't in imminent danger of freezing to death - so what better way of protecting her from freezing to death? Put blubber on!

Janet's subconscious had continued to protect her in this way for many years. The moment she started to lose some of the blubber when dieting, she would feel anxious. She wouldn't know why she felt anxious as she didn't *consciously* know about the freezer incident. Her subconscious, however, would work to sabotage the diet, and Janet would pile the weight back on.

When this memory surfaced in my consulting room, Janet said what most clients say at this point: 'What on earth made me forget about that? I can remember it as though it happened yesterday! I can remember how frightened/guilty/ashamed (whatever the emotion was that was too overwhelming to deal with) I felt.'

Janet went on to continue with all the 'now-I-know-whys': 'Now I know why I never shop in the frozen food store. I always felt anxious if I had to be near those freezers. Now I know why I am always cold, even in the middle of summer. Now I know why I always wear two vests. Now I know why I never eat meat.'

Now, at last, this memory could grow up. Now it could have logic and reason added to it. Now her subconscious could stop trying to protect her by keeping the blubber on.

Without the need to diet Janet found many changes taking place for her over the next few months as the pounds melted away. Her metabolic rate increased, so she had more energy. Her tastes began to change. Things she liked before she no longer liked, such as cream cakes, ice cream, fried fish and chips and other such fatty or sugary foods. Things she didn't like before she now found herself enjoying, such as crisp fresh vegetables and so on. She developed a craving for sparkling mineral water, even though she had previously told herself she would never pay money for water.

Janet lost six-and-a-half stone, and her weight has remained steady ever since. She is very happy about her weight, her shape and herself.

Margaret

Margaret was a rather timid woman, 42 years old and about four stones overweight. When I regressed her, this is what surfaced.

Margaret had had a friend called Debbie whom she had known

since their school days. They had spent a lot of time in each other's houses and were more like sisters than friends. One day, Margaret had been at Debbie's house making a cup of tea when Debbie's fiancé James, had come into the kitchen and made a pass at her. Margaret had been unable to handle this situation. You or I might have been able to control the situation quite easily, but Margaret was timid and shy. She had felt she couldn't tell Debbie, as Debbie might be hurt, or might not believe her. Margaret couldn't face the possibility of losing her best friend. Neither could she stand up to James.

How could her subconscious protect her in a case such as this? It could make her fat and unappealing to the young buck.

This her subconscious had continued to do, even though Margaret had long since lost touch with her friend.

Once I had regressed Margaret and unlocked the underlying problem, she then gradually lost the excess four stone.

Edna

Edna, rounded and short, was an elderly client of mine. She began therapy in the usual way - I taught her self-hypnosis and instructed her to visualize herself as she wished to be. She then went to Australia for a few months to visit her son. She made an appointment with me on her return, and I was expecting to have to instruct her all over again, as I assumed she would have abandoned self-hypnosis while on holiday and would not have progressed with her weight loss. Edna arrived at my consulting rooms and I was stunned to see that she now resembled a Barbie doll. Her entire body was slim, except for her breasts, which were as big if not bigger than when she first began the therapy. I suggested we continue with therapy to discover why her subconscious had not removed fat from her breasts.

'Don't you dare,' she replied. 'I had more fun on the beaches in Australia with these big things than I have ever had in my life!'

Edna's subconscious knew exactly what it was doing. This is how she had been visualizing herself, and this is what it had produced. Who says you can't slim just the parts you want smaller?

Chapter Twelve

Other Uses for Self-hypnosis

As you reach your ideal body weight, you may be interested in making further self-hypnosis tapes to improve other areas of your life. You might wish to increase your self-esteem, improve your confidence, overcome stress, etc. using the information and skills you have now learned.

You already have at your fingertips all you need to make your own scripts, and I do advise you to do so, since you know, better than anyone else, what *you* need to improve in *your* life. If you would prefer some guidelines, however, take a look at the scripts in this chapter.

You will see that all of these incorporate the notion of *weightlessness*, to help further program your subconscious mind to encourage more rapid weight loss as you are working on other aspects of your life. **Remember, first the mind changes, then the body.**

When making your tapes, use the same **Induction** and **Deepening** script as given in Chapter 8. Substitute the following scripts, or adaptations of these scripts you make for yourself, for the **Positive Suggestions and Imagery** given in Chapter 8. *Always* (unless, of course, you are making a tape for insomnia) include the usual **Waking Up** routine. For insomnia, eliminate the Waking Up segment and just allow yourself to drift off to sleep.

Confidence or Self-esteem Building

Positive Suggestions and Imagery

As you relax more and more deeply, your subconscious mind is to the fore ... ready to help you to improve your life in many ways. In the days and weeks ahead, more and more your thoughts will dwell on all you have achieved in your life to date. Begin by taking a few moments to recall as many achievements as you can ...

Imagine a rainbow ... Imagine yourself weightless, floating along the rainbow ... sliding down the rainbow as it arches through the sky

... and imagine you have reached the end of that rainbow ...

Imagine, there, in a hollow in the ground, at the end of that rainbow, is an empty pot ... For each thing you have so far achieved put a piece of gold into that pot ... First the big pieces for big things, and then the little pieces for smaller things, acknowledging that all are worth while ...

[Having allowed plenty of time for memories of all your achievements to surface, during the next few minutes use any of the following suggestions or 'prompts' which might be appropriate to you, again pausing between each one for it to sink in.]
a)putting your children's needs first so many times
b)learning to read, to swim, to drive a car, to handle money and manage day-to-day finances
c)creating a child or children/creating life
d)succeeding against all odds
e)keeping going when many others may have given up
f)helping others in so many ways

Think for a moment of all the obstacles you have overcome in your life, and what you have learned from those obstacles ...

[Add any special achievements of which you are proud.]

As you become happier with yourself that happiness spreads to all who know you. They bathe in your smile, your confidence, your laughter, your joy, your happiness ... And now accept that you are a very special person with your own unique way of thinking about things. Your own unique way of doing things ...

Think for a moment of all the millions of people that have preceded you on this planet and know that not one of those people was exactly like you ... This is how unique and special you are ...

Think of all the millions of people who will succeed you on this beautiful planet called Earth and know that not one of those people will have the same talents and way of thinking about things that you have ... Love that uniqueness, that specialness that is yours alone ... and you now give away any need to 'follow the herd' ... And you will no longer judge yourself against others because you know you *are special and unique ... as you drift deeper and deeper.*

This new-found inner strength enables your confidence and self-assurance to grow day by day ... Day by day, many things will improve in your life ... your income, your home life, your calmness, your confidence, your health, your vitality, your fitness; all growing day by day. Your abilities and special talents and qualities grow stronger day by day as you recognize your true worth
as you drift deeper and deeper.

Your health improves day by day ... You become stronger, fresher, fitter, healthier ... Each day and every day you become happier ... happier with yourself, happier with life and happier with the people around you ... And you now enjoy that uniqueness that is yours alone ... As you become happier day by day, energy fills your body ... like a bubble of joy getting bigger and bigger ...

Think for a moment of all the obstacles you have overcome ... as you drift deeper and deeper.

Think of all the things you have achieved ... as you drift deeper and deeper and deeper still ... feeling so good about yourself, and your life, and about all you have created and will create in the future ...

[*Slowly introduce the Waking Up script.*]
Stress Control

Positive Suggestions and Imagery

As you have learned to relax so well, in the days and weeks ahead, anytime you wish to relax you will be able to do so, easily, naturally and effortlessly ...

Anytime you feel stressed ... anytime you feel anxious ... anytime you simply want to relax ... you will be able to do so, easily, naturally and effortlessly, no matter where you are and no matter what you are doing ... with your eyes open, or with your eyes closed ... by simply taking those three very slow ... very deep breaths ... holding each breath ... and, on the exhale, saying to yourself the word 'relaaaax' ... You will instantly become calm and relaxed and able to handle any situation, more effectively from that calmness ... from that relaxation ... and with total calmness and confidence in yourself ...

Things, people, events that could previously tense, upset or annoy you will now simply calm and relax you ... Friends and acquaintances will be amazed at the calm and efficient way you now handle situations that previously were stressful ... Whenever you feel tense, irritable, or anxious, you will think of those three slow, deep, breaths and immediately become calm, relaxed and totally confident in yourself and your abilities ...

Visualize yourself in a situation that previously would have been stressful to you ... Now take three very slow ... very deep breaths ... Hold each breath ... and, as you breathe out, just say to yourself the word 'relaaaaax' ...

Now imagine yourself again in that same situation and notice how you now handle that situation with calmness and with total confidence in yourself ... Things, people, events that used to make you feel tense and anxious ... will now calm and relax you ... They will simply flow over you ...

Imagine yourself in another situation that previously would have made you feel tense and anxious ... Now take those three, long, slow, deep breaths and, as you become calm and confident, imagine yourself handling that same situation in a much more calm and relaxed way ... a more efficient way ...

Imagine a box ... a strong, sturdy box ... with the lid open ... Put all your worries, troubles, problems, hurts, stresses and anxieties into the box, one by one ... If there are any thoughts in your mind at this moment that are preventing you from deeper relaxation, put those into the box too ... Just let them go now ... If there is any part of you which is trying to do anything ... let it go into the box as well ... Just let go ... Now close the lid and lock it all away ... As you close the lid, feel the calmness and peacefulness spreading throughout your body ... The box is now yours to keep for the rest of your life ... Nobody knows you have this box as it is locked safely in your subconscious mind ... anytime in future that you may start to feel stressed ... anytime you feel anxious ... anytime you simply want to relax ... you will be able to do so, easily, naturally and effortlessly ... by simply closing your eyes and imagining your box ... You will be able to put all that stress, all that tension, all that anxiety into your box ... close the lid, and lock it all away ... And each time you do this you will immediately become calm, peaceful and relaxed and able to deal with any problems with calmness and total confidence in yourself ...

You will probably find, when you eventually go back to your box to deal with those problems, that most of them will have disappeared. Most of them will have melted away, but any stubborn ones that may remain you'll simply deal with, with calmness and with total confidence in yourself ... This is your own secret, safe problems box ...

And as you have learned to relax so easily, so completely, you're going to find that after a few times of playing this tape or disc, you have a very calm feeling inside ...

When all around you are tense and anxious, you'll be the calm one ... the relaxed one ... You'll have a calm, self-assured feeling, a bright, hopeful feeling, an optimistic feeling inside ... a relaxed feeling, a 'looking forward to life and what it brings' feeling ... with calmness and with total confidence in your ability to deal with any challenges that life brings ... And this calm, confident self-assurance ... this peacefulness ... is going to persist and remain with you ... And the very situations which previously would tense and irritate you will now simply flow over you, enabling you to enjoy life as it was meant to be enjoyed ... to the full ...

Now let yourself drift ... let yourself sink into that calm feeling ... And for the next little while just enjoy feeling calm and relaxed ... and allow your thoughts to do whatever they want to do ... Allow whatever thoughts want to drift into your mind to just be there ... Almost as an observer, watch those thoughts, whilst feeling calm and relaxed ... It is as if those thoughts belong to someone else and you are simply watching them without judgment or criticism ... Just watching ...

Drift and float in that calmness ... that peacefulness ... Wrap that calm, peaceful, feeling into a sort of lazy bubble and tuck it inside yourself ... somewhere safe inside yourself ... and you will carry that bubble with you long after you finish playing this tape/disc ... You will carry it with you into the days and weeks ahead ... feeling it as a sort of calm, peaceful glow deep inside you ...

[Introduce the Waking Up script.]

For practical tips on putting together your own self-hypnosis tapes, see Conclusion on page 71.

Conclusion

You now have all the knowledge you need to make hypnosis recordings for yourself.

There are many ways you can improve your life using self-hypnosis and, as only *you* know what *you* wish to change in your own life, it is impossible to discuss the principles of making the tapes in anything other than general terms. I will, however, give you some useful advice to enable you to make tapes successfully:

1. What Is Expected Tends to Be Realized
If you listen to your tape telling yourself 'It will not work for me' / 'I can't relax enough' / 'It is going to take a long time for it to be effective' / 'It won't work if I am disturbed while playing the tape' / 'I am different from everyone else so I will be one of the few with repressed material in my subconscious' (or any number of similarly negative thoughts), then your results (or lack of them!) will reflect this. For example, if you tell yourself you are never going to get to sleep tonight, what happens? Insomnia!

If, on the other hand, your thoughts dwell more on the positive aspects, such as 'I am going to lose three pounds a week' / 'I am doing very well' / 'I now sleep deeply every night', then, again, this is what will happen. As I said before, the brain is very powerful when used to the full.

2. Always Use the Present Tense
'I am now the perfect body weight for my height' / 'The pounds are simply melting away' are the kinds of things you need to say, rather than 'I will be slim soon', because your subconscious does not know what time span is meant by 'soon', so is unlikely to create what you want it to.

3. Set a Time Limit
Sometimes it is impossible to convince yourself that what you want to create can occur immediately. In this case, introducing a time limit can help. For example: 'I will have the confidence to make a speech at the Golf Club Christmas dinner on December 14th.'

4. Suggest Action, Not Ability to Act

For example, don't say 'I have the ability to dance well' but rather, 'I dance well, with ease and grace.'

5. Be Specific

It is not much use to your subconscious to say, 'I would like to be ten stone but I would be happy with ten and a half, though I really should be nine and a half, but ten would be good.' Your poor subconscious simply does not know what to program from this. Keep it literal, keep it specific - and reap the rewards!

6. Keep Your Language Simple

Do you know what the acronym KISS stands for? 'Keep it simple, stupid.' The state of hypnosis does not lend itself to having to think or work things out. If you have to do these things, you are using conscious mind and bringing yourself out of hypnosis - which defeats the object.

7. Exaggerate and Emotionalize

Use descriptive words like 'wonderful', 'exciting', 'great', 'thrilling'. Your subconscious will respond to these.

8. Use Repetition

Imagine your mind is like a six-year-old child. Repeat phrases over and over again. First time you are likely to listen with your conscious mind, but as the phrase is repeated constantly through the script, your conscious mind knows what is coming so shuts down with boredom and your subconscious mind takes over (hypnosis).

9. Be Positive

If you say, 'My headache will be gone when I come out of hypnosis' you are suggesting a headache. It would be more effective to say, 'My head feels better and better. It is clear and relaxed. My head feels good! It will continue to feel good after I come out of hypnosis, because all the nerves and muscles are rested, relaxed and functioning normally.'

10. Never Mention the Negative Idea You Intend to Erase

Instead, as mentioned above, repeat and emphasize the positive idea you are replacing it with.

11. Do Not Attempt to Judge

Just accept that when you have completed the count from ten down to zero you are in hypnosis. Again, if you judge, you are using your conscious mind and bringing yourself out of the state you are trying to create.

Well, here it is, the end of the book! I hope you have enjoyed reading it as much as I have enjoyed writing it. Use it well: it can provide you with all the skills you need to be happier and healthier for the rest of your life.

Useful Addresses

Training organizations with lists of fully qualified hypno-analysts in your area, available on request:

The National Council of Psychotherapists
David Doohan
PO Box 6072
Nottingham
NG6 9BW
(01159) 131382
www.natcouncilofpsychotherapists.org

International Association of Hypnoanalysts
Robert Kelly
PO Box 417
Cambridge
CB2 1WE
(01762) 261181
www.hypnoanalysis.com

I would also welcome any feedback you care to give about this book: e-mail address: trisha25742@aol.com

WEEK 1: Record everything you eat and drink

MONDAY	TUESDAY

WEEK 1: Record everything you eat and drink

WEDNESDAY

....

....

....

....

....

....

....

....

....

....

....

....

....

....

....

THURSDAY

....

....

....

....

....

....

....

....

....

....

....

....

....

....

....

WEEK 1: Record everything you eat and drink

FRIDAY	SATURDAY	SUNDAY

WEEK 2: Record everything you eat and drink

MONDAY	TUESDAY
....	....
....	....
....	....
....	....
....	....
....	....
....	....
....	....
....	....
....	....
....	....
....	....
....	....
....	....
....	....

WEEK 2: Record everything you eat and drink

WEDNESDAY

THURSDAY

WEEK 2: Record everything you eat and drink

FRIDAY	SATURDAY	SUNDAY
....	....	....
....	....	....
....	....	....
....	....	....
....	....	....
....	....	....
....	....	....
....	....	....
....	....	....
....	....	....
....	....	....
....	....	....
....	....	....
....	....	....
....	....	....

WEEK 3: Record everything you eat and drink

MONDAY

TUESDAY

WEEK 3: Record everything you eat and drink

WEDNESDAY	THURSDAY

WEEK 3: Record everything you eat and drink

FRIDAY	SATURDAY	SUNDAY
....	....	....
....	....	....
....	....	....
....	....	....
....	....	....
....	....	....
....	....	....
....	....	....
....	....	....
....	....	....
....	....	....
....	....	....
....	....	....
....	....	....
....	....	....
....	....	....

Further Reading

Having read this book, listened to the CD and achieved your ideal bodyweight you may well be wanting some assistance with what to eat to help maintain your health. A healthy diet is more than just balancing food intake, it involves eating foods that promote rather than endanger health. What are the elements of a healthy balanced diet? How do we identify which are good fats, bad fats and essential fats? What problems can be caused by sugar in our diet? What are the different types of sugars found in our diet and which are healthy? What should we drink and what should we avoid drinking? What essential supplements do we need? The answers to these questions and many more are contained in *Your Lifestyle Diet* written by Karen Sullivan and also published by Wellhouse Publishing. The introduction to this book is reproduced on the following pages for your information.

Introduction

It often takes a health scare to make the majority of us look at our eating habits. And although many of us are aware that our diets are not all they should be, few of us make any real attempt to redress the balance. We have supermarkets full of good, fresh food, but most of us choose the easy options - ready-made meals, take-aways, fast food, junk food and snacks eaten on the run. The concept of healthy eating sounds rather laborious and tasteless, and who has time to prepare nourishing meals? What's more, everyone else appears to eat much the same kinds of food, without any apparent ill-effects, so why make changes when there seems to be no need?

The fact is that what you eat affects your health much more dramatically than you might imagine.

Food forms the building-blocks of every single system, cell and bone in our bodies, and it affects the way they work and renew themselves. While most of us can get away with an unhealthy diet for a while, there's no doubt that over time we will begin to pay the price. Here are just some of the reasons why:

- A joint report by the World Cancer Research Fund (WCRF) and the American Institute for Cancer Research (AICR) claims that 30-40 per cent of cancers may be caused by dietary factors.

- According to a study published in *The Lancet*, average sperm count in Britain fell from a high of 113 million per millilitre in 1940 to 66 million in 1990. If this trend continues we can expect infertility to become a mass epidemic by the middle of the 21st century. A huge number of studies show that nutrition is the main cause, with oestrogens in the water, our food and in the environment playing havoc with male fertility. Men with low vitamin C also have a markedly increased likelihood of genetic damage to their sperm. You may be past the point of wanting to start a family, but it's worth considering what the future holds for our children, and our children's children.

- The British Heart Foundation says that more than 300,000 people in the UK suffer a heart attack each year, and of those, 115,000 die. Heart disease is the number-one killer in the UK. Apart from smoking and lack of exercise, the main cause is diet. You might also be interested to learn that some 20 per cent of children show early signs of heart disease, again caused by diet. This is not a problem for the older generations alone.

- Osteoporosis (thinning of the bones) is a condition that normally affects the elderly, but studies show that low bone mass (bones that are not strong enough) is becoming more and more common in younger members of society. This poses a great personal risk, but also affects the nation as a whole, as the cost of caring for disabled members of society skyrockets.

- Consider, too, what the food you are eating is doing to your body. Processed foods have little nutritional value and contain a huge number of chemicals, the effects of which are only just beginning to be made clear. Many additives have now been banned, but some - particularly tartrazine or E102 - have been linked to hyperactivity in children, allergies, asthma, migraines and even cancer. Scientists are investigating a possible link between aspartame (found in diet drinks) and changes in brain function. Caffeine is linked to peptic ulcers, insomnia, nervousness and birth defects.

- Don't forget the problems associated with overweight. Half the population of the UK is now considered to be clinically overweight (that number is even greater in the US), and the numbers are increasing dramatically. Overweight presents a serious risk to health, and common related conditions include high blood pressure, high cholesterol, an enlarged heart, diabetes and a much higher risk of heart disease.

And there's more. Many of us are unaware that the niggling health complaints from which we suffer, such as headaches, fatigue, PMS, sleep and skin problems, aches and pains, digestive disorders, memory problems, trouble conceiving, mood swings and even menopausal symptoms, are related to the food we eat. A poor diet means that everything in our bodies works less efficiently, and in a less balanced way. Unless we get the nutrients we need, in fresh, wholesome food, we will be heading down the slippery slope towards serious health problems.

In an age where self-help books are top of best-seller lists around the world, it's hard to work out why such a very basic component of health and wellbeing is being neglected. And believe me, it is. A new study claims that only 13 per cent of men and 21 per cent of women in the UK manage to eat the daily recommendation of five portions of fruit and vegetables, and sales of biscuits, crisps and other processed foods are on the increase. Many people do not bother with breakfast, and a recent survey shows that a huge number of people skip meals because of the frantic pace of their lives. The research, by the supermarket chain Sainsbury's, found that nearly 70 per cent of people regularly miss at least one meal a day. Six out of ten people surveyed said they were simply too busy to stop to eat.

One factor influencing our eating habits is obviously the overscheduled nature of our lifestyles. The prospect of preparing a healthy, nutritious meal after a busy day at the office, or while dealing with screaming kids, is a daunting one. In the end, we adopt a measure of self-preservation, cutting corners when we can. One of the areas that is most affected by this approach is our diet. And there are thousands of manufacturers and retailers lining up to meet the demand for instant meals that can be prepared with a minimum of fuss.

We've also adopted a rather extraordinary cost-cutting mentality when it comes to food. We demand cheaper food in larger quantities, a trend that has seriously lowered the overall quality of the food on offer.

But good food is a necessity, not a luxury, and by lowering the overall standard, we are further undermining our diets and our health.

There are a multitude of myths surrounding healthy eating, and most of them go back to just a couple of decades ago. Healthy eating brings to mind, for many of us, pulses, unpalatable 'whole' breads, boiled greens, muesli and an array of tasteless, unidentifiable vegetables. And fair enough. With a limited repertoire of cooking styles, an absence of ethnic influences and a restricted number of foods available, 'health food' was indeed something that the majority of consumers would want to avoid.

But all that's changed. We have fresh, interesting and exotic foods flown in from halfway around the world; we have exciting international chefs who have transformed healthy eating into an art form; we have a vast array of ingredients, from a wide variety of cultures, all available in local supermarkets. What's more, there are reputable manufacturers now producing appetising, healthy fare at reasonable prices. We can buy woks and omelette pans that make preparation easy, and we have microwaves, food processors, juicers and steamers to do much of the work for us. In fact, there is simply no excuse for opting out of the healthy eating revolution. We are talking delicious food that makes us look and feel good, and we can prepare it in much the same time that it takes to plonk a few ready-made meals into the oven.

And that's what this book is all about. Healthy eating is more than just a short-term trend for a few health-conscious individuals. It comprises a revolution in the way we view our lives and look after ourselves. It holds the key to a healthy, happy future, in which we experience the type of good health and wellbeing that all of us deserve. It's called *Lifestyle Diet* because healthy eating should be just that - a normal part of a healthy lifestyle.

It's easy to eat well, no matter what your budget or tastes. Once you understand the very basic concepts behind the elements that make food good or bad for us, you will find a whole new world opening up to you. Choosing, preparing and eating good food can be a sublime experience, and make a real difference to the way you feel.

There are no major life changes required in making the shift to healthy eating. With a little knowledge, the transition is easy. But like anything else in life, the more energy you give it, and the bigger a priority it becomes in your life, the more you will benefit. And in just a few short weeks, you'll begin to look and feel better than you may have felt in quite some time. Your future is in your hands, and it's up to you to grasp it.

DIVERTICULITIS

Dr Joan McClelland

Diverticulitis is a Cinderella disorder. It is very common, can be dangerous and there are rapidly increasing numbers of sufferers. We stand a more than 50 per cent chance of suffering from diverticulitis before we reach the age of 60. Dr Joan McClelland describes in her easily accessible style the symptoms, different types of diverticulitis, complications and various treatments including alternative and herbal remedies. This book also covers the psychological aspects of diverticulitis and the benefits of exercise and diet.

ISBN: 1-903784-00-X   128pp

ANXIETY AND DEPRESSION

Beth MacEoin

We live in stressful times and have to cope on a daily basis with a variety of different pressures. These can include financial worries, emotional stresses, bereavement, break-up of relationships and insecurity at work. When feeling well and resilient we are able to cope with a wide range of these stressful situations. It is when we become mentally and emotionally overloaded at a vulnerable time in our lives that we can suffer from symptoms of anxiety or depression. Beth MacEoin describes in her easily accessible style the various symptoms and suggests a wide range of practical measures to provide positive support.

ISBN: 1-903784-03-4   128pp

HOW TO COPE SUCCESSFULLY WITH

CANDIDA THE DRUG-FREE WAY

Jo Dunbar

Candida is the common name for an overgrowth of yeast organism known as *Candida Albicans*. Candida appears with many seemingly unrelated symptoms – it affects almost every part of the body and has become an umbrella term for any collection of symptoms of no identified cause. Because of the wide range of symptoms and the lack of positive diagnostic tests available, this gap has provided fertile ground for individuals of limited medical training to quickly hop on the band wagon and begin 'diagnosing' Candida for almost any condition or illness. This book introduces a thorough drug-free treatment program, as well as tips on how to adapt your life-style to treating Candida.

ISBN: 1-903784-11-5

128pp

HOW TO COPE SUCCESSFULLY WITH

COLITIS

Dr Tom Smith

We know a lot about the changes that occur in the bowel of people with colitis and how to return them to normal. It should be only a matter of time before we know *why* these changes happen. Colitis means 'inflammation of the large bowel' (the colon), inflammation takes several forms and doctors have different views from the general public on what constitutes colitis. Most of this book is devoted to ulcerative colitis and Crohn's, with chapters on how to distinguish these inflammatory bowel diseases from irritable bowel, diverticular disease and colon cancer.

ISBN: 1-903784-12-3

128pp

HOW TO COPE SUCCESSFULLY WITH

CROHN'S DISEASE

Dr Tom Smith

Although on Crohn's disease, this book compares the similarities and differences to ulcerative colitis. Dr Smith describes how modern medicine is used to relieve and prevent serious complications. He explains how the normal bowel works, how it can go wrong and why it can produce the three main symptoms of diarrhoea, bleeding and mucus. This book describes the tests, investigations, and the diagnosis of the illness. It is not just the illness but how much of the bowel is infected that affects the treatment and how quickly and completely recovery is made. Other bowel problems that mimic Crohn's are described.

ISBN: 1 903784 16 6   112pp

HOW TO COPE SUCCESSFULLY WITH

DEPRESSION

Dr Tom Smith

In his easily accessible style Dr Tom Smith describes depression and explains why we get depressed, the treatment with drugs together with other treatments. It shows how to think through your depression, what you can do for yourself and how to change those negative thoughts, become more outward going and assertive together with sleep problems. Depression is a serious illness that needs serious attention. Everyone in the family doctor's team has to help, the sufferer's family must also be aware of the risks and how to give assistance. Dr Tom Smith describes in this book the help you can get.

ISBN: 1903784 14 X   112pp

HOW TO COPE SUCCESSFULLY WITH

HIGH BLOOD PRESSURE

Dr Duncan Dymond

Blood Pressure is not a disease, everyone has a pressure, we need it to keep us upright and alive. Your blood pressure varies depending on your level of physical and mental stress. In this easily accessible book Dr Dymond describes what high blood pressure is, the symptoms, various medications available, side effects and possible complications. The tests and investigations for high blood pressure are explained together with treatments and suggestions for changes to lifestyle and diet.

ISBN: 1-903784-07-7   128pp

HOW TO COPE SUCCESSFULLY WITH

HIGH CHOLESTEROL

Dr Tom Smith

We are all becoming more aware of high cholesterol problems and often only discover that we are at risk when having a geneneral health check. In this book Dr Tom Smith describes in his easily accessible style the causes of high cholesterol, the associated problems, the complications and the risks involved if your high cholesterol goes untreated. Dr Tom Smith details the treatments available together with possible side effects. He also gives information on diet and lifestyle changes which may be needed to help reduce your cholesterol levels and reduce the risks to your overall health.

ISBN: 1-903784-09-3   128pp

HOW TO COPE SUCCESSFULLY WITH

IRRITABLE BOWEL SYNDROME

Richard Emerson

Irritable Bowel Syndrome is a complex problem with both physical and psychological symptoms. The aim of this book is to set out clearly and concisely these symptoms and the various treatments now available – conventional, complementary and alternative. Ths should enable sufferers to improve their lifestyle and either cure or manage their Irritable Bowel Syndrome.

ISBN: 1-903784-06-9   128pp

HOW TO COPE SUCCESSFULLY WITH

MENOPAUSE

Dr Joan McClelland

The menopause is an event to welcome, a stimulating new chapter in your life. You can say goodbye to period pains, water retention, PMS together with a host of psychological problems including irritability, depression and chronic tension. The menopause is a vantage point from which to take stock, reviewing your earlier life and looking ahead to new interests, deepening relationships and fresh goals. You are entering an important and fascinating time in your life and to get the best out of it you need to work in harmony with nature, this book aims to help you achieve this aim.

ISBN: 1-903784-05-0   128pp

HOW TO COPE SUCCESSFULLY WITH

PANIC ATTACKS

Karen Sullivan

Panic attacks are a much more common problem than is generally realised an affect a large proportion of the population. They can manifest themselves in many ways including agoraphobia, anticipatory anxiety, separation anxiety, school or work phobia. This book explains what Panic Attacks are, the causes, how panic affects daily life and the associated disorders. Conventional treatments together with their side effects are explained and alternative remedies including acupuncture, homoeopathy, reflexology, massage are covered. Karen Sullivan gives reassuring short term measures to help deal with an attack and, together with other advice, Top Ten Tips to help cope in the longer term.

ISBN: 1-903784-08-5

128pp

HOW TO COPE SUCCESSFULLY WITH

SLEEPING WELL - THE DRUG FREE WAY

Beth MacEoin

Good sleep is an important part of your total health. There is no uniform pattern to sleep problems, a great deal depends on an individual's make-up. Problems include difficulties in switching off, frequent waking and a sense of being unrefreshed on waking. Other factors may be over-reliance on caffeine, alcohol or chemical sedatives. Bad working habits can play a large part in preventing sound sleep. This book contains positive strategies to solve these problems and break the negative cycle. The major systems of alternative medicine included in this book have a different perspective to conventional medicine on the issue of sleep problems.

ISBN: 1 903784 13 1

128pp